ARTIFICIAL LIFE
POSSIBILITIES:
A *STAR TREK* PERSPECTIVE

D1478190

ARTIFICIAL LIFE POSSIBILITIES:

A *STAR TREK* PERSPECTIVE

PENNY BAILLIE-DE BYL

CHARLES RIVER MEDIA, INC.
Hingham, Massachusetts

Cover Design: Tyler Creative

CHARLES RIVER MEDIA, INC.
10 Downer Avenue
Hingham, Massachusetts 02043
781-740-0400
781-740-8816 (FAX)
info@charlesriver.com
www.charlesriver.com

Penny Baillie-de Byl: *Artificial Life Possibilities: A* Star Trek *Perspective.*
ISBN: 1-58450-414-5

This book is printed on acid-free paper.

Baillie-de Byl, Penny.
 Artificial life possibilities : a Star Trek perspective / Penny
Baillie-de Byl.
    p. cm.
 Includes bibliographical references and index.
 ISBN 1-58450-414-5 (pbk. : alk. paper)
 1. Artificial intelligence. 2. Artificial life. I. Title.

Q335.B33 2006
576.8'3—dc22
                        2005033577

Printed in the United States of America
05 7 6 5 4 3 2 First Edition

CHARLES RIVER MEDIA titles are available for site license or bulk purchase by
institutions, user groups, corporations, etc. For additional information, please contact
the Special Sales Department at 781-740-0400.

Contents

Preface

A t the time this book was being written the world saw the cancellation of *Enterprise*, the fifth incarnation of the *Star Trek* television series. This conjures up a sense of deja vu in fans everywhere when they think back some 39 years to the axing of Gene Roddenberry's original *Star Trek*. Back then it was fans that brought it back, fuelled by the creative inspiration radiated by the series.

This inspiration has fuelled the passion of not only arm chair fans, but also of researchers out there on the coal face of technology, developing the devices of the future, aiming to better the human race and struggling to conquer space travel. This is illustrated in a timely way by the $3 million (U.S.) donated to TrekUnited (the organization attempting to get Enterprise back on air) by commercial space flight industry investors, who say that Star Trek has inspired at least one out of two of all entrepreneurs in the space flight industry (*www.saveenterprise.com*). This same inspiration has also emerged as a series of commentary books on Star Trek physics, technology, and even metaphysics. And this book is no exception.

Inspired by the many computerized characters on *Star Trek*, this book is an examination of these artificial intelligences. Admittedly, if you look at AI today it is a far cry from the sophistication of Data and the Emergency Medical Hologram (EMH); however, we are looking at beings that people imagine will exist around 300 years from now. Driven by the inspiration of the *Star Trek* dream, we endeavour to ask the questions, *Will we make it? Will we have best friends who are androids?* and most importantly, *Will we be upgrading our home theatres for Holodecks?* We, along with many other Trekkers, hope so. This book has been written to provide both the serious Trekker and the occasional voyeur a handbook of the current techniques and devices available in the fields of artificial intelligence, robotics, and artificial life. We examine the development of artificial life forms such as Data and the EMH from the bottom up, including their physical creation and programming, to determine if such beings might some day be a reality.

Just as the original *Star Trek* series was reincarnated due to pressure from fans, let's hope we can do it again. What Paramount needs to understand is that *Star Trek* is not *just* a television show. It is inspiration.

Although we have attempted to give an even coverage of all *Star Trek* series, the author is particularly familiar with *The Next Generation* and *Voyager* and thus more examples are taken from these series. In addition, as Data and the EMH are of particular interest, it seems only natural to focus on these series. Each episode referenced in the book is identified by series and name. The convention we use, found on *www.StarTrek.com*, is to abbreviate the series as follows: *TOS = The Original Series, TNG = The Next Generation, DSN = Deep Space Nine, VOY = Voyager*, and *ENT = Enterprise*. In addition, the movies are referenced by name and the movie number. For example, *Insurrection*, the ninth *Star Trek* movie, is referenced as *STIX: Insurrection*. We have also attempted to be a little clever by incorporating Star Trek episode titles as the section titles within the chapters. Some of them fit well with the content, some require a little imagination as to why we selected them, and some.... well they were the best we could find! If the titles don't seem to enlighten the content we hope you will forgive us and enjoy reminiscing about the particular episode's content instead.

Our ability to predict the viability of the *Star Trek* future herein is obviously clouded by a current day *technological singularity*. In the field of futurology, this is a predicted point in our development that we do not have the ability to fully comprehend progressing beyond. We hope that 24th century readers will forgive our level of insight.

Acknowledgments

Foremost I would like to thank my family, Daniel, Tabytha, and Deefa, for their continued support during this arduous journey. Watching so many episodes of *Star Trek* in such a short time and retaining one's sanity would be difficult for any hard core Trekker. Their unwavering assurance in my abilities is appreciated.

Thanks must also go to the anonymous reviewers of the various drafts of this book for their constructive feedback and suggestions. In particular, I would like to thank my good friends Sian and Mark Carlyon and Chris Mills for their reviews and input. May you *live long and prosper.*

Next, I would like to show my appreciation for the confidence my publisher, Jenifer Niles, puts in my ability as a writer. This is the second time she has taken on my ideas and for that I am truly grateful. This book has been the culmination of ten years of watching *Star Trek* and writing bits and pieces. Being able to finally put it all together is the fulfilment of a dream.

To the various academics and writers I have referenced throughout the book, a special thanks. Without your contributions to the fields of robotics, artificial intelligence, A-Life, and specific understanding of the human mind, such a book would not have been possible.

Finally, to Gene Roddenberry, thank you for the inspiration.

The Journey Begins

THE ASSIGNMENT (*DSN#504*)

Imagine for a moment we have been propelled into the 24th century. World peace, no famine, cures for all types of nasty diseases, and people working to better themselves for the sake of it rather than wealth. This was the dream of Gene Roddenberry[1] which is perpetuated by the *Star Trek* writers and many of us who share this vision of the future. As intriguing as their ideas are, just how insightful are they? To answer this question we will be taking a journey of reverse archaeology. Rather than looking at the past and contemplating how life must have been, we will be considering the *Star Trek* future and discussing how life could be. Let's imagine we have visited the 24th century and have returned to contemplate how the journey from our present time might progress.

"But!" I hear you thinking, "*Star Trek* isn't real."[2] Although you might be onto something, we unfortunately do not possess the ability to travel forward in time to see how things will turn out. Often we rely on the wild imaginations of writers and forward thinkers such as Issac Asimov, Jules Verne, and Leonardo da Vinci to inspire our technological development. We like to think of Gene Roddenberry in the same light. His unbound dreams of the future, beginning some forty years ago and continuing to the present day through an impressive team of science fiction writers, have inspired research into technologies such as warp drive, transportation, holographics, lasers, robotics, artificial intelligence, and hyper sprays. Little did Roddenberry know when he described his visions as containing tech-nobabble[3] that others with real scientific skills would be inspired to make them a reality. Therefore, in lieu of Captain Braxton's 29th-century Federation timeship *Aeon* (*VOY*: "Future's End Parts I and II"), we are only limited by our imagination of what the 24th century will hold. However, rather than devising a vision of the future here, how much more fun to examine a view of the forthcoming confined within a fictitious universe with some 40 years of history.

As the *Star Trek* future contains far too many ideas for us to philosophise about in one book, we will limit our discussion to the field of Artificial Intelligence (AI) with which we are particularly familiar and passionate[4]. The question we will be asking throughout is, "How do we get from where we are now to the point where we are able to create truly exceptional artificial beings such as Holodeck characters, Lieutenant Commander Data, and the Emergency Medical Hologram?" In order to answer this, we need to examine where we are right now and extrapolate where we are heading. This book integrates a passion for *Star Trek* with academic research from the AI, A-Life, and Robotics domains and presents it in an easy to understand way, bypassing the technobabble and mind blowing mathematics. It examines the characteristics and capabilities of *Star Trek*'s artificial life forms and compares them with current technologies in an attempt to predict if we will ever create such advanced beings. If you have ever wanted to know what a positronic brain is or how to write a personality subroutine, then this is the book for you!

THE ULTIMATE COMPUTER (*TOS#053*)

Trying to answer the question *What is artificial intelligence?* can be more trouble than it is worth. The problem is that because we (all humans) consider ourselves to be intelligent beings, we all have an opinion on what it means to be intelligent. This becomes very evident when you attempt to find a definition of intelligence in either the AI or psychology domains and are faced with a plethora of vagueness, inconsistencies, oversimplification, overspecialisations, contention, and downright stubborn opinions and short-sightedness. In 1921 a journal asked 14 prominent psychologists and educators to give a definition of intelligence. The journal received a different definition from each person. In 1986 researchers repeated the task with 25 experts and received a similarly diverse range of answers.

Some psychologists contend that intelligence is not a feature of the human mind but the result of how the brain processes information. This is no better illustrated than in *VOY*: "Message in a Bottle," when the Emergency Medical Hologram (EMH) is sent on a mission to the Alpha Quadrant and *Voyager* is left without a chief medical officer. To fill in while the doctor is away, Harry and Tom decided to create a new EMH. The EMH's holographic matrix programmed by Harry looks exactly like the real thing.

Harry then downloads *Gray's Anatomy*[5] into its database. After adding a few vocal subroutines, the replica EMH begins reciting the text word for word. Not exactly what Tom had in mind. What this shows is that although the replica EMH looked human, sounded human, and had extensive anatomical information in its database, it did not have the capacity to process that information in a useful way. If the replica EMH was to take the information from *Gray's Anatomy* and fix an injured crewman's broken leg, then we might say it exhibited intelligent behaviour.

Psychology aside for the moment, the problem with most definitions of artificial intelligence is that they blatantly relate machine intelligence to human intelligence. This may seem a little naive when talking about the 24th century, where we have apparently encountered other species with intelligence far greater than our own. The *if it acts like a human* mentality just won't cut it. There are many instances in *Star Trek* when an intelligent being is encountered and yet does not behave in the way you would expect a human to behave. Defining AI in terms of human intelligence disallows us from recognizing artificially intelligent beings with intelligence superior (or even inferior) to our own. Not only this, but as we cannot clearly define what our own intelligence is, it is very difficult to use it as a gauge for judging the performance or characteristics of something else.

If you aren't an AI aficionado, to give you a taste of some of our frustrations, here are but a few definitions of AI:

- an effort to make computers think [Haugeland85]
- automating activities associated with human thinking [Bellman78]
- creating machines that perform human intelligence level functions [Kurzweil90]
- to make computers perform tasks that humans are currently better at [Rich91]
- the ability to achieve human-level performance in cognitive tasks [Turing50]
- the automation of intelligent behaviour [Luger93]

And the list goes on. It's not that these definitions are not useful, but that they try to define a form of intelligence in terms of intelligence. In a way, this leaves the identification of artificial intelligence solely to the discretion of the individual making the assessment.

This provides us with another problem. How do we identify intelligence? Can it be measured? As we all have some intuitive idea of what intelligence is (since we apparently possess it) we often tend to provide a qualitative description of another's intelligence using terms such as clever, smart, dumb, street smarts, genius, stupid, and gifted. In addition, these terms are not used to describe some kind of general intelligence but a whole range of types of intelligence. For example, one theory of intelligence lists seven types: logical-mathematical, linguistic, musical, spatial, bodily-kinesthetic, interpersonal, and intrapersonal [Gardner89].

Another point of view is that intelligence is something that varies in value between cultures. For example, most western cultures associate verbal and mathematical skills with intelligence, whereas smaller island cultures value spatial memory and sea navigating skills. In the same way, in the *Star Trek* universe, Klingons would rate bodily ability as a superior intelligence where as Vulcans would regard logical intelligence more highly.

This means that any type of standardised testing for the existence of general intelligence is highly subjective and possibly irrelevant. Take, for example, the Intelligence Quotient (IQ) test. This is maybe the oldest and best known test in psychology for measuring intelligence. The IQ test determines a person's mental abilities relative to others of the same age. It does not make allowances for a person's cultural background or differing types of intelligence. In the 1970s and 1980s in California, thousands of African-American children were assessed using a standard IQ test (used on Anglo-American children) as being mentally retarded and were placed into special education programs. After a massive court battle it was determined that some of the 20 tests that were being used improperly measured these children's abilities and the tests were thus banned.

Taking all this into consideration, we seek a definition of intelligence that can help us identify the characteristic in others, not only biological but also machine. It must focus on the individual's abilities and objectives, and, although possibly compared with our own, provide some unbiased objective conclusions about the individual's mental abilities.

Adapted from [Fritz97] we will define intelligence as follows: a being's level of performance in reaching its objectives.

What does this mean for our artificial friends? Taken literally, if the preceding is our definition of intelligence, then an artificial intelligence should be a *produced*[6] *rather than natural intelligence*; hence our use of the word *machine* or *computer* in AI.

Captain Picard throws a wrench in the works of our definition. His revelation that *we are all machines* in *TNG*: "The Measure of a Man," when he compares Data's construction with that of humans, gives us something further to consider. Where do we draw the line between *natural* and *produced* beings? Although we consider ourselves to be natural, were we not produced, regardless of that production being a biological process? If an intelligent machine creates another intelligent machine, is this new machine considered artificially intelligent? When humans procreate, the baby is not considered artificial, and, in the same sense, if a machine creates another machine in its own image, then it is not artificial relative to its parent, as in the case of Data's daughter, Lal, in *TNG*: "The Offspring." In the *Star Trek* universe, when photonic beings from the 5th dimension invade *Voyager*, in *VOY*: "Bride of Chaotica," they consider the artificial EMH to be as natural as themselves. Might we also take this further and consider a race of mechanical beings who have biological computers and debate their computers' ability to be intelligent? It just depends which side of the fence you sit on or in which galaxy or dimension you originate.

It is therefore not the embodiment of a being that determines whether or not it is intelligent. As per our definition, intelligence is a factor of performance. Therefore, just being a computer or a machine does not make for an artificial intelligence. Data is not an artificial intelligence; he is an android who possesses artificial intelligence. In the same light, the EMH is a hologram who possesses artificial intelligence, and Seven of Nine is a human who possesses elements of artificial intelligence thanks to her Borg implants. When Picard argues that we are all machines, he makes the very point that our physical construction is irrelevant when comparing abilities of the mind.

We now offer our definition of artificial intelligence as follows: an enhancement of the cognitive abilities beyond those inherently/naturally present in a being or device for the use of achieving its objectives.

For example, today the run of the mill, everyday personal computer does not possess artificial intelligence. It can, however, be programmed with such abilities to help boost its performance. The same can be said of Seven of Nine. She already possesses natural human intelligence; however, her Borg implants help to boost her mental abilities.

Now that we have a definition of AI, we can examine what new abilities it brings to or enhances in a being. These are the very characteristics found in the most agreed upon definitions of intelligence from both the AI and psychology domains. They include

- the ability to adapt to new situations;
- the ability to engage in abstract and original thinking;
- a capacity for knowledge acquisition;
- a capacity for independence; and
- an ability to judge and reason.

When we think about AI in relation to *Star Trek*, we tend to think about beings with holistic intelligence and full embodiments. However, today, the term AI is more frivolously tossed around. You may have heard of, or even owned, electronic devices that use AI to better their operation. In fact, you can buy microwave ovens which have a *Fuzzy Pizza* button that will reheat cold pizza to perfection. In this example, the manufacturers have created a device that can reheat any piece of pizza, regardless of weight, temperature, or toppings, with the press of only one button. This may make the oven appear intelligent as it can detect the state of the inserted pizza and cook it accordingly. The term *fuzzy* in this context is used to address a field of AI known as *fuzzy logic*. This is an area that attempts to calculate some distinct final value from a range of vague (or fuzzy) values. In the case of the oven, it cannot possibly know what is on the pizza but it can estimate[7] its weight and temperature and come up with a cooking time and temperature setting. If you think the only fuzzy things in *Star Trek* are tribbles [*TOS*: "The Trouble with Tribbles" and *DSN*: "Trials and Tribble-ations"], catch up with the discussion on fuzzy logic in Chapter 7.

According to Russell and Norvig [Russell95], today's AI can be defined as machines[8] that fall into one or more of four categories: machines that think like humans, machines that act like humans, machines that think rationally, and machines that act rationally. You may be wondering why the distinction is made in these categories between *human* and *rational*. First, it does not suggest that humans are not rational. It merely makes the allowance for rational thought and behaviour to exist outside the realm of human cognition and activity. It means that we recognise that humans are not the *be-all-and-end-all* of intelligent life. This is a particularly good start if we are suggesting the existence of alien races other than our own in the *Star Trek* future.

With all this in mind, let's examine today's categories of AI with respect to some artificial beings in *Star Trek*. We will also eliminate the first two categories relating specifically to human beings and assume they become subsets of the remaining.

Machines that Think Rationally

As with both of these categories, in order to understand the types of machines that fit within, it is necessary to appreciate the category itself. What does it mean to *think*? You may think this is rather subjective and open to much debate, like the topic of *intelligence*. In the field of AI, however, to *think* refers to systems that, when given a problem, can come up with the plausible solutions. By plausible, we mean something that seems reasonable to an observer. In order to determine if a machine is thinking, we need to have a better understanding of our own thought processes. The two ways to achieve this are introspection, or examining the way we think, or through psychological experiments. Once we have formulated theories on how we *think* we think, we can program them into a computer and observe its behavior for similarities with humans or other beings we consider to be intelligent. Some experiments in AI are not concerned with the computer coming up with the correct answer, but are more interested in the steps it takes to reason about the problem it is given. By the term *think*, we actually mean *compute*. Therefore it is not enough for a machine to appear to be thinking, it must actually go through the motions. To the untrained eye, a holodeck character might be classified as intelligent, just by the fact that it can take on humanoid shape. It can also appear animated, including simulated breathing, talking, walking, and eating. While some holodeck characters may in fact possess intelligence, the ones we might consider *extras*[9] are simply following scripts and are no more intelligent than the replica EMH we spoke about in the previous section.

The exocomps introduced in *TNG*: "The Quality of Life," not only appear to be thinking, but actually are thinking. The exocomps are an intelligent work tool designed by Dr. Farallon with which she can communicate via a remote control. They have the ability to adapt by forming new circuit pathways in their artificial brains. Dr. Farallon had been using the exocomps to build a *particle fountain*, an orbital station that can mine a planet's surface from space. When Dr. Farallon informs an exocomp of a fluctuating antimatter flow converter via its remote control communication device, the exocomp's response is to replicate a mode stabiliser to fix the problem. Geordi la Forge's response to the exocomp's decision is "Very nice," and thus confirms his belief that the exocomp made a reasonable decision about solving the given problem in line with what he himself might have come up with.

Machines that Act Rationally

To act rationally means to behave in a way that achieves one's goals. In 1967, Koestler proposed that rational human action was motivated by two ultimate goals, *self preservation* and *preservation of the species*. Self preservation is the goal by which a human acts to stay alive. Activities motivated by this goal might include eating, earning money, or running from a targ[10]. Preservation of the species is a slightly less selfish goal, motivating acts such as saving another's life or procreating. If we use these two goals as guidelines for the motivation of rational behaviors, how do the exocomps measure up?

In *TNG:* "The Quality of Life," when Dr. Farallon sends one of the exocomps into a conduit to seal a plasma manifold, the exocomp enters the tube and promptly returns without completing its work. Dr. Farallon is puzzled by its behavior and attempts to program it to go back into the conduit. Data, who is watching the process, observes that the exocomp is ignoring the doctor's commands. When she attempts to override the exocomp's control processor, she receives an electric shock from the exocomp's remote control. Soon after, the conduit the exocomp had just exited explodes. Dr. Farallon, Data, and Geordi examine the malfunctioning exocomp back aboard the *Enterprise*. They soon discover that the circuitry in the main unit that connected the exocomp with the remote control had completely burned out. On further investigation, they also discover the exocomp's new circuit pathways have increased by 632%. Dr. Farallon informs Data and Geordi that this is not the first time she has witnessed such a phenomena and that it signifies the exocomp has malfunctioned beyond repair. When Geordi asks Data if he knows what made the conduit explode, Data responds that the conduit had a microfracture undetectable to their instruments. Geordi concluded that it was good luck for the exocomp that it happened to malfunction at that time.

Following these events, Data becomes concerned that the exocomps have evolved into sentient[11] creatures because of their apparent fear of death and postulates that the exocomp didn't malfunction but detected the microfracture and thus exhibited a survival instinct. He is concerned that they are not allowed to express their free will and are being used as slaves. For the moment, whether or not the exocomp is actually sentient is not our concern. That it acted on a self-preservation goal is.

Later, Captain Picard and Geordi are trapped on the particle fountain when a radiation leak prevents them from transporting back to the *Enterprise*. The state of the particle fountain means they have only 22 minutes before they are mortally exposed. Dr. Farallon suggests the exocomps be programmed to explode inside the particle stream to shut the station down. Data strongly objects to this plan and locks down the transport system to prevent Dr. Farallon transporting three exocomps into the particle stream. Data says he will release the transport system if the exocomps are allowed to make the decision to be transported. When the exocomps are given a choice, they come up with a different plan to get Picard and Geordi back to the *Enterprise*. On transporting to the particle fountain, the exocomps begin extracting power from the station to disrupt the particle stream enough to transport Picard and Geordi away from danger. Once they achieve their objective, the *Enterprise* attempts to transport the exocomps back. Unfortunately only two are retrieved. Data concludes that one has stayed behind and disrupted the particle stream to save the others. This is an excellent demonstration of not only the *preservation of the species* goal, but also a concern for others not of their own kind.

PROTOTYPE (*VOY#129*)

Artificial intelligence has come a long way since its inception in the 1930s. Here are some of the milestones that have paved the way.

1936   Alan Turing publishes the paper *On Computable Numbers, with an Application to the Entscheidungsproblem*. This article sets the limits of computer science and introduces the Turing Machine, an abstract machine that provides a precise definition of a computational processes.

1942	Isaac Asimov specifies the three laws of robotics in the book *I, Robot*: 1) a robot may not directly or indirectly harm a human being; 2) a robot must obey the directions of a human being except in the case where the orders conflict with 1; and 3) a robot must always protect itself, except where this rule conflicts with 1 and 2.
1943	Warren McCulloch and Walter Pitts publish *A Logical Calculus of the Ideas Immanent in Nervous Activity*. This article describes how neural networks learn.
1950	The game of chess is analyzed for the first time as a searching problem by Claude Shannon.
1950	Alan Turing devises the Turing test. A machine that passes the Turing test is said to be able to convince a human interrogator that it is actually human.
1956	The term *artificial intelligence* is invented by John McCarthy at Dartmouth College, New Hampshire.
1956	The first AI program, Logic Theorist, is demonstrated by Allen Newell, Cliff Shaw, and Herbert Simon at the Carnegie Institute of Technology. The program could solve thirty-eight of the fifty-two mathematical theorems in Whitehead's and Russell's book *Principia Mathematica*.
1956	Maniac I, the first chess program to beat a human player, is created by Stanislaw Ulam.
1959	Arthur Samuels develops a checkers-playing program with the ability to defeat human players.
1965	Herbert Simon, joint winner of the A.M. Turing Award for basic contributions to AI in 1975, predicts that machines will be capable of doing any work a man can by the year 1985.
1966	ELIZA, a computer program which parodies a Rogerian therapist, is created by Joseph Weizenbaum. This program is classified as the world's first chatbot.
1969	The Stanford Research Institute in California develops Shakey, a robot exhibiting skills in locomotion, perception, and problem solving.
1975	Genetic algorithms, first conceived in Germany in the 1940s, are explained in the book *Adaptation in Natural and Artificial Systems* by John Holland.

1979	Hans Moravec at Stanford University creates a computerized autonomous vehicle that successfully negotiates a chair-filled room.
Mid-1980s	Neural networks become a popular area in AI research.
1997	Garry Kasparov, world chess champion at the time, is beaten by the Deep Blue chess program.
1997	Microsoft's Office Assistant (*that paperclip!*), uses AI to help the user.
1999	NASA's Deep Space 1 spacecraft is controlled by an AI called Remote Agent for two days, 100 million kilometers from Earth.
2001	The unmanned Global Hawk aircraft is fully navigated by an AI navigation system to guide it on a 13,000-kilometer journey from California to Australia.
2004	All contestants in the DARPA Grand Challenge to build an intelligent vehicle that can navigate a 229-kilometer course in the Mojave desert fail to complete the course.
2005	Cyc to go online. Cyc is an AI attempting to assemble a complex database of everyday common-sense knowledge with the objective of being able to replicate human-like reasoning.

LITTLE GREEN MEN (*DSN#480*)

The field of Artificial Life (A-Life) investigates the scientific, engineering, philosophical, and social issues involved in our ability to synthesize life-like behaviors from scratch in not only computers and machines, but also in molecules and other mediums.

These studies allow researchers to push the boundaries in the understanding of *life-as-we-know-it* and go beyond to examine *life-as-it-could-be* (*www.alife.org*). Topics that fall into the domain of A-Life include biological organization, the origin of life, self-assembly, growth and development, evolutionary and ecological dynamics, animal and robot behavior, social organization, and cultural evolution [MIT05].

A-Life is about understanding the relationship between low-level rules and high-level behaviors. For example, A-Life considers how the simple interactions between birds in flight lead to their complex yet elegant flocking patterns, and how simple ant behavior can cause remarkable trails with intricate shapes and structures. In the A-Life community, it is hoped that through the understanding of these systems, novel solutions to complex real-world problems, such as disease prevention, stock-market prediction, and data-mining on the Internet, can be found [Adami98].

One of the most interesting areas in the A-Life arena is the construction of living systems out of non-living parts. There are two focus groups working in this area. The first is attempting to create self-replicating molecules using the classical biological building blocks of carbon-based life, and the second is simulating populations of self-replicating entities via a computer. Both are endeavoring to uncover the secrets to the origin of life.

Yet another area of A-Life, and the one we are particularly interested in, is working towards creating truly adaptive autonomous robots. The work in A-Life robotics differs from the undertaking in traditional robotic domains in that the emphasis is on building robots that can interact with their environment in order to learn and adapt.

We will now take a look at some specific areas and applications that fall into the A-Life realm.

Cellular Automata

Cellular automata are simple system models studied in some areas of mathematics. You may have seen them before but not known exactly what they were called. In a simple form, cellular automata consist of a regular two dimensional grid of cells containing values which are called states. When drawn, the state of a cell is usually depicted by its color. The initial state of the cellular automata is often established by randomly setting the values of the cells. Illustrated in Figure 1 is a cellular automata 10 by 10 cells, where the possible values for the cells are 1 or 0, displayed as black or white respectively.

The values of all cells are updated in one iteration. The new value a cell takes on depends on the values of its neighboring cells and other specified functions. Depending on how the cells are updated each iteration, certain patterns begin to form in the grid.

The most famous cellular automata is Conway's Game of Life. The updating function for the cell values is thus:

- a dead cell (with a value of 0) with exactly 3 live neighbors becomes alive (set to 1).
- a live cell (with a value of 1) with 2 or 3 live neighbors stays alive; otherwise it dies (set to 0).

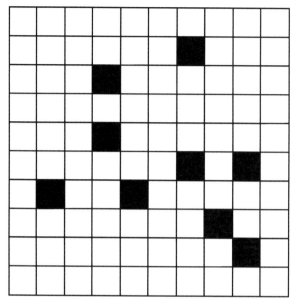

FIGURE 1 A cellular automata with two possible cell states; 1 or 0. In such systems, cells with a value of 1 are called alive, and with a value of 0 are dead.

The first six states for the Game of Life are shown in Figure 2. It illustrates how an initially random system can become organized using simple rules. It is difficult to appreciate the beauty of such a system using still images. Suffice it to say, the randomness of the initial system evolves into repeating animated patterns.

The patterns found in the game of life are so common that they have been assigned special and poetic names. Some of these patterns are shown in Figure 3. They include static patterns, called *still lifes*, that form and do not change whilst their neighboring border remains dead; *oscillators*, which are similar to still lifes with the exception of a part that appears to be animated, similar to the hands of the clock shown in Figure 3 (b); and *spaceships*, which seem to fly across the grid. For a greater appreciation of the Game of Life in action, see the java applets available at *www.generation5. org/content/ 2003/alifejava.asp.*

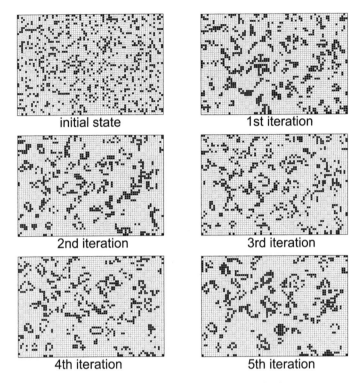

FIGURE 2 The first five iterations for a Game of Life.

Other patterns that have been discovered in the Game of Life include *guns*, which remain stationary and shoot out spaceships; *puffers*, which fly like spaceships leaving a path of debris; and *rakes*, which are like puffers but emit spaceships. It truly is difficult to gain an appreciation of the Game of Life without seeing it in action.

Another fascinating cellular automata is that of Chris Langton's *Ants*. It features a single ant which moves about on the grid changing the state of the cells. The ant follows three simple rules:

1. The ant moves forward in the direction it is facing.
2. If the ant lands on a black square, the square turns white and the ant turns 90 degrees right.
3. If the ant lands on a white square, the square turns black and the ant turns 90 degrees left.

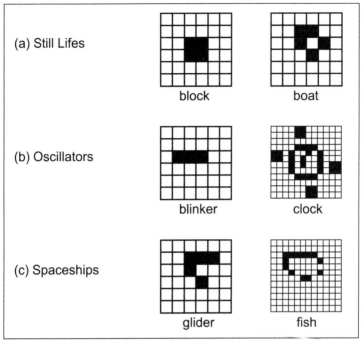

FIGURE 3   Some patterns found in the Game of Life. (a) Still Lifes, (b) Oscillators, and (c) Spaceships.

From what seems like a very erratic beginning, the ant ends up forming an elegant pattern of complex pathways and connecting clumps. Some iterations of this cellular automata are shown in Figure 4.

Simulations

Some cellular automata could, in a sense, be classified as simulations of real world systems; however, there are some models that are more sophisticated and not restricted to a grid world. The aim with A-Life simulations is again to produce realistic models of real world systems using simple atomic rules.

One example of such a simulation is that of the flocking behavior in birds. Craig Reynolds, a prominent figure in the SIGGRAPH animation and A-Life fields and winner of the 1998 Scientific and Engineering award for pioneering work in three-dimensional computer animation for motion pictures, was first to develop flocking techniques. His methods have

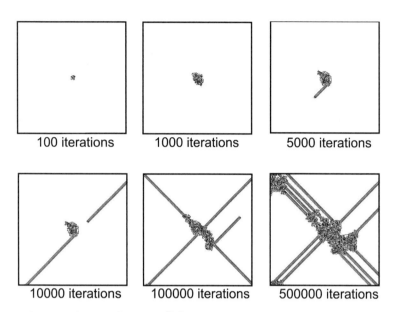

FIGURE 4   Langton's *Ants* cellular automata.

been used in movies such as *The Lion King* and *The Mummy*. Starting with a flock of randomly moving virtual birds, each one is subjected to three rules:

1. Don't get too close to the other birds.
2. Always steer towards the flock's average heading.
3. Always steer towards the flock's average position.

Although very simplistic, the rules produce an excellent simulation of flocking birds. Several frames of this simulation are shown in Figure 5.

Another type of simulation is that of evolution. In these types of systems, a world is populated with a set of creatures that exhibit simple behaviors such as hunting, eating, procreating, and staying alive. One such A-Life simulation is Jason Spofford's Primordial Life, where artificial life forms called *boits* evolve in a two dimensional environment in a battle of survival. A screen shot of this simulation, available from *www.io.com/~spofford/index.html*, is shown in Figure 6.

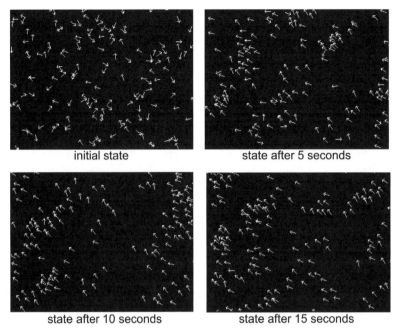

initial state   state after 5 seconds

state after 10 seconds   state after 15 seconds

FIGURE 5   Twenty seconds of Craig Reynolds' flocking A-Life.

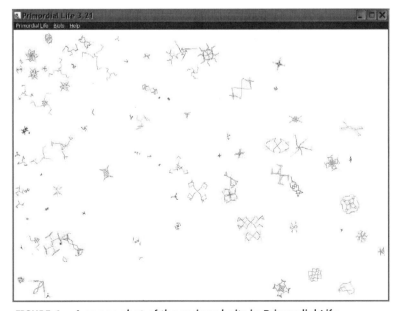

FIGURE 6   A screen shot of the various boits in Primordial Life.

Most simulations of this kind which involve a breeding process between life forms implement special programs called genetic algorithms. We will learn more about these in Part II.

THE STORYTELLER (DSN#414)

Obviously Data and the EMH are the first characters to come to mind when talking about AI, A-Life, and *Star Trek*. However, given the previous sections, specific examples begin to emerge from the storylines involving these characters and others that help us better define their intelligence and life-like qualities. The following classifies events throughout *Star Trek* where particular focus is given to the characteristics of AI and A-Life.

TOS: "**What are Little Girls Made Of?**" This episode is the first in which artificial intelligences are examined in *Star Trek*. A long-lost exobiologist, Dr. Roger Korby, is located on Exo III. The doctor has learned how to build androids by studying the technology of the long-extinct inhabitants of the planet. The *Enterprise* crew is amazed at the human-like appearance and behavior of the androids.

TOS: "**The Changeling**" A probe called Nomad sent out from Earth in 2002 is found melded with an alien device that is hell-bent on destroying anything that is imperfect. Its mission is the result of its original programming to seek out new life with the integration of the alien device's program to sterilize soil samples.

TOS: "**I, Mudd**" The *Enterprise* is apprehended by an android named Norman pretending to be a crew member, and taken to a planet where Kirk's nemesis Harry Mudd is being kept against his will. The planet is inhabited by androids designed by an extinct race. The androids saw Harry's arrival as a blessing and were devoted to fulfilling his every need. With a new purpose having been found since the expiration of their original creators, they are reluctant to let Harry leave.

TNG: "**Encounter at Farpoint**" Data is the first android character introduced into the main *Star Trek* cast.

TNG: "**The Offspring**" Data creates a daughter named Lal, modeling her on his own physical structure. Starfleet wants to take control of the new android, but Lal wants to stay with her father on the Enterprise. Unlike Data, Lal experiences unexplained strong emotions under the threat of being removed from Data's presence. These emotions eventually lead to neural collapse and her death.

TNG: "**Elementary, Dear Data**" A Holodeck recreation of a Sherlock Holmes-type mystery brings forth a new sentient life form depicted by the character Professor Moriarty. Due to La Forge's command to make the character a worthy adversary of Data, Moriarty is programmed to be aware of his existence. Dr. Moriarty returns in TNG: "Ship in a Bottle" and demands to be set free from his holodeck confines.

TNG: "**The Quality of Life**" When Dr. Farallon introduces the Enterprise crew to the intelligent work tools called exocomps, Data becomes convinced that they are sentient when they exhibit self preserving behaviors and free will. Data puts Captain Picard and La Forge's lives at risk when he refuses to send the exocomps on a suicide mission to save them. Instead, the exocomps are allowed to make their own decision and come up with a plan to save both humans.

DSN: "**His Way**" Dr. Bashir introduces the Deep Space Nine crew to his more than ordinary holographic friend, Vic Fontaine, a Las Vegas lounge singer from the 1960s. Vic has been programmed to be fully aware of the nature of his existence. Vic is instrumental in getting Odo to reveal his real feelings for Major Kira and counseling Nog through the post traumatic stress of losing a leg.

VOY: "**Caretaker**" The first sentient holographic crew member is introduced as the Emergency Medical Hologram on Voyager when the human doctor is killed. He becomes an invaluable member of the crew, expanding beyond his original programming to deal with new alien species and pursue creative interests such as operatic singing.

VOY: "**Dreadnought**" When Voyager discovers a Cardassian guided missile heading towards a populated planet in the Delta Quadrant, Chakotay and Torres own up to having reprogrammed the missile in the Alpha Quadrant but are perplexed as to why it is still active and targeting an innocent race. B'lanna has programmed the intelligence of the missile so well that she has a difficult time convincing it she isn't under Cardassian coercion and that the missile's sensor readings are incorrect.

VOY: "**Warhead**" Harry brings a crashed device apparently suffering from a machine form of amnesia on board Voyager. When the device remembers that it is a warhead with a mission to destroy a planet, it abducts the EMH's physical embodiment and demands Voyager help it complete its mission.

The preceding list is by no means an exhaustive record of the artificial intelligences that appear in *Star Trek*, but does provide us with a good overview.

THE STRUCTURE OF THIS BOOK

Our initial intention for this book was to examine all of the artificial intelligences that appear in *Star Trek* in order to cover the vast domain of AI and A-Life. However, as we progressed through the contents we soon discovered that the main artificial beings, Data and the EMH, provide more than enough material to investigate the feasibility of their existence. You will therefore find that most of the material herein focuses on these two characters. Having said this, there is the odd occasion where other AI examples from *Star Trek* pop up to clarify an example.

This book has been structured into three parts: *Body*, *Mind*, and *Soul*. Part I, Body, presents the physical nature of artificial beings. In the case of Data, we examine the building of androids, the structure and capacity of his positronic brain, and the way in which he perceives his environment. For the EMH, we take a look at the nature of holograms and whether or not a hologram with the same physical parameters of the EMH could exist. In Part II, Mind, we go into the theory behind programming intelligence into machines. We look at the nature of logic and the storage of knowledge, and examine some well known AI programming structures such as artificial neural networks and genetic algorithms in the hope of giving the reader a taste for programming AI subroutines. Finally, Part III, Soul, covers some metaphysical aspects of the *Star Trek* AIs and attempts to find answers to their abilities of developing relationships with others, experiencing emotions, getting creative, and being funny. We hope you enjoy your journey through this book and gain some inspiration and appreciation for the Star Trek universe and the field of artificial intelligence.

REFERENCES

[Adami98] Adami, C., 1998, *Introduction to Artificial Life*, Springer-Verlag Inc., New York.

[Koestler67] Koestler, A. 1967, *The Ghost in the Machine*, Penguin Books Ltd., London.

[Luger93] Luger, G. F. & Stubblefield, W. A., 1993. *Artificial Intelligence: Structures and Strategies for Complex Problem Solving*, Benjamin/Cummings, Redwood City, California, second edition.

[MIT05] MIT Press, "Artificial Life", available at mitpress.mit.edu/catalog/item/default.asp?sid=57384B50-8974-4207-A193-0EF3F54527E2&ttype=4&tid=41&xid=13&xcid=4364, March, 2005.

[Russell95] Russell, S, and Norvig, P., 1995, *Artificial Intelligence: A Modern Approach*, Prentice Hall, Upper Saddle River.

[Turing50] Turing, A., 1950, Computing Machinery and Intelligence, in *Mind*, vol. 59, pp. 433-460.

[Gardner89] Gardner, H. & Hatch, T., 1989, Multiple Intelligences Go To School: Educational Implications of the Theory of Multiple Intelligences, *Educational Researcher*, vol. 18., no. 8., pg. 6.

[Fritz97] Fritz, W., 1997, Intelligent Systems and Their Societies, New Horizons Press, available at www.intelligent-systems.com.ar/intsyst/index.htm, January 2005.

ENDNOTES

1. Star Trek's creator.
2. Wash your mouth out!
3. Ironically told to the founding father of Artificial Intelligence, Marvin Minsky.
4. The author's fields of scientific research cover artificial intelligence and believable computer game characters.
5. An exhaustive anatomical reference on the human body first written in 1918 by Henry Gray.
6. Taken from the definition of *artificial*.
7. The oven cannot know for sure if you have added weight to the pizza by placing it on a plate, how the weather might be affecting the temperature it reads from the pizza, or if the inserted object is indeed a pizza.
8. Russell and Norvig use the term *system* rather than *machine*. We feel that to make the distinction between artificial and real, the term *machine* is a better fit.
9. Likened to extras in movies.
10. A wild boar native to the Klingon homeworld.
11. Self-aware or has a conscience.

PART I

Body

CHAPTER 1

Positrons, Neurons, and the Android Brain

CHAPTER OVERVIEW

In this chapter, we examine the structure and capacity of Data's positronic brain and discuss the potential for such a computing device to someday exist. Fortunately, the *Star Trek* writers have given us a lot of technical specifications to examine which assists in our investigation. We start by looking at the inspiration behind the technology in Data's positronic brain, and then examine current machine processing and storage technologies and theories about how these will evolve in the future to extrapolate the plausibility of creating a processing unit equal to or greater than that given to Data.

GENESIS (*TNG#271*)

In 1932 the American physicist Carl Anderson discovered the *positron*. Little did he know the implications that this subatomic particle (similar to an electron but with a positive charge) would have for science fiction. The term *positronic* first appeared in the writing of author Isaac Asimov. In 1940, Asimov began writing stories about robots. By sheer accident he also invented the word *robotics*. In search of a unique yet scientifically plausible way of describing the construction of an artificial brain, he dreamed up the *positronic brain*. Asimov, who described the artificial brain as having "enforced calculated neuronic paths," was the first to admit that the concept was total baloney. However, the term, which was original and futuristic at the time, seems to have become indispensable in the *Star Trek* universe.

According to *Star Trek* history, in 2336 Dr. Noonien Soong of the Omicron Theta colony constructed two intelligent androids with fully-functional positronic brains. The first of these androids is introduced in *TNG:* "Encounter at Farpoint" as Lieutenant Commander Data. He is the only android to have ever been given full legal human rights. Dr. Soong also created a twin version of Data (often referred to as his "brother")[1], whom we come to know as Lore in *TNG:* "Datalore." Apparently Lore is different to Data in one respect: Lore has emotions. We will further explore what emotions mean to artificial beings in Chapter 11. These emotions make Lore extremely dangerous and motivate the colonists on Omicron

Theta to shut him down. The colony at Omicron Theta is then destroyed by the Crystalline Entity. Data survives this attack and is rescued by Starfleet.

Data's positronic brain is the physical structure that supports his neural network. Once an idea in a science fiction writer's imagination, the *artificial neural network* (ANN) is now a reality and has been for some time. When Asimov described the positronic brain as having "enforced calculated neuronic paths," he wasn't far from the truth. We will explore the nature of ANNs further in this chapter. Suffice it to say that a complex ANN is capable of working on only one problem at a time, for example, visual face recognition. For each problem-solving task, Data would require a separate neural network.

Imagine building a set of ANNs with all the capabilities that Data exhibits. Not only would you have to consider Data's visual recognition abilities, but also other senses such as smell, touch, sound, and taste. Furthermore, recognition isn't the only use for an ANN. It can also determine how Data behaves in different situations and how he remembers things. It should make your brain hurt just thinking about it. Although you can't get a true idea of the immense task building such a complete ANN would be without reading ahead, at this point just believe us when we say it would be monumental!

PRIME FACTORS (*VOY#110*)

Data's positronic brain not only consists of an artificial neural network that can process information, but it also has two properties that are common to all computers: storage and speed. The absolute storage capacity of his positronic brain is 800 quadrillion bits, and his total computation speed is approximately 60 trillion operations per second. This sounds very impressive for the size of his brain. But considering the size, storage, and speed of today's computers and the rate at which they are evolving, will it be possible by 2335 (the approximate year of Data's creation) to achieve this capacity?

Peak Performance (*TNG#147*)

Both the storage and speed of computers is based primarily on the number of transistors that can be put onto an integrated circuit. For the computer illiterate, you can call it a computer chip. An integrated circuit is basically a complete electronic circuit built into a small chip made of silicon (hence the term silicon chip). A transistor is a device that amplifies a signal or opens or closes a circuit. A specific type of integrated circuit called a microprocessor represents the brain of a computer. The microprocessor is where most of the computer's processing is performed. A typical microprocessor about the size of one square inch can contain tens of millions of microscopic transistors.

In 1965, Gordon Moore made the observation that since the invention of the microprocessor in the early 1950s, the number of transistors per square inch has doubled with every year. At the time, Moore predicted this trend would continue into the foreseeable future. After his initial observation the development of microprocessors slowed down a little, so the doubling of transistors occurred every 18 months instead of every year. This doubling prediction is known as Moore's law and is shown in Figure 1.1. With the doubling of transistor density also comes the doubling of data density or the size of the storage capacity of the chip.

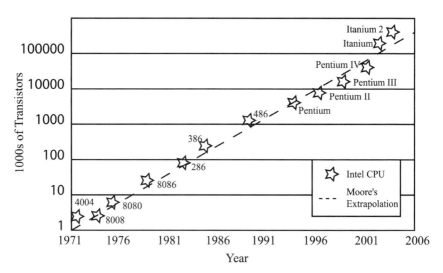

FIGURE 1.1   An extrapolation of Moore's Law with an overlay of Intel chip releases.

The first-ever microprocessor was Intel's 4004. Although this chip was only able to add and subtract, it was the first time in history that a computer's processing functions were integrated onto the one chip. Before this, computers were built from collections of chips or individual transistors wired together. The 4004 powered one of the first portable electronic calculators. It was capable of processing 4 bits at a time.

Investigations (*VOY#135*)

Before continuing, we should probably give you a quick overview of what a *bit* is so that you will be able to appreciate the amount of information that is manipulated by a computer. Basically, one bit is the storage of a 0 or a 1. Why just 0 and 1? Why not 0, 1, 2, 3, 4, etc.? Put simply, an electric switch can be in either of two states, off or on. Imagine a lamp plugged into the wall. When you flip the switch in one direction the light goes on. This indicates that electricity is flowing into the lamp. When you flip the switch in the other direction, the light goes off. This indicates that the electricity is no longer reaching the lamp. This is the very foundation that a computer is built on. Think of the computer as thousands of little switches. Each switch can be in one of two states, off or on. When the switch is off, it represents a 0, when the switch is on, it represents a 1. The single 0 or 1 is called a bit.

Because a bit can only have the value of 0 or 1, it is pretty useless for representing data with more than two values; therefore, bits are grouped together. The 4 bits processed by the 4004 are called a *nibble*. Group 8 bits together for a *byte*. The number 10100011 is a byte of bits, because there are 8 digits in it. Representing numbers as a series of 0s and 1s in this way is called *binary*. Each digit in the binary number represents a number in decimal. Each of these decimal values can be added together to determine the decimal number that is represented by the binary number. In binary, each digit represents a different value of *2 to the power of* some other number. The right-most digit represents 2 to the power of 0 (2^0). Moving to the left, the next digit represents 2 to the power of 1 (2^1). And so it goes. Here is a simple example. Given the binary number 10100011, you can determine the decimal number that it represents by considering the value of each digit. The easiest way to do so is to draw up a simple table displaying the *2 to the power of* values and then placing the binary number in it. This can be seen in the table in Figure 1.2. For each column in the table where there is a one, the corresponding decimal column values are added together to determine the answer. In this example, 10100011 binary is equal to 163 decimal.

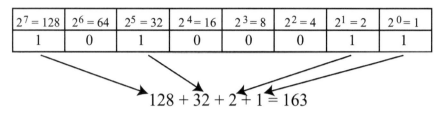

$2^7 = 128$	$2^6 = 64$	$2^5 = 32$	$2^4 = 16$	$2^3 = 8$	$2^2 = 4$	$2^1 = 2$	$2^0 = 1$
1	0	1	0	0	0	1	1

$$128 + 32 + 2 + 1 = 163$$

FIGURE 1.2   Conversion of a binary number into decimal.

Setting each bit's value to 1 would represent the largest number that can be stored in a specific number of bits. In a single byte, the largest number would be represented by eight 1s or 11111111. This number, when converted to the decimal system would be 256.

The first byte-sized chip (8 bits), Intel's 8086, was the first chip to make it into a home computer. The chip was integrated into IBM's first PC (Personal Computer). It could process 0.64 million instructions per second (MIPS). In 2000, the latest personal computing microprocessor from Intel was the Pentium IV. It was capable of processing around 1700 MIPS. This was certainly a vast improvement on the old Intel 8086. Today microprocessors are not usually rated in MIPS because of the number of the differing instruction cycles needed to perform basic operations in different chips. Due to this, the Standard Performance Evaluation Corporation has created a number of tests used to rate the chips (called benchmarking) that results in two performance measurements. The first type examines the number of whole number (integer) calculations that can be performed per second. The second type looks at the number of floating-point operations per second (FLOPS). This measurement examines the number of calculations the chip can perform with fractional values in a second. One FLOP is equivalent to the chip doing an addition or multiplication. The Intel 386 chip used 59.5 instruction cycles to perform just one FLOP, whereas the latest Intel Itanium can perform the same process in 1.3 cycles. The number of FLOPS for the chip will then depend on how fast the chip performs a cycle. Suffice it to say, there is much debate in today's computing power environment on exactly how a chip's performance should be measured. It is no longer as simple as it was in the early 1990s.

IN THEORY (*TNG#199*)

But what does all this have to do with Data's brain power? Well, in order to predict if it might be possible to build a computer capable of processing 60 trillion operations per second (or 60,000,000 MIPS) by the year 2335, we need to examine trends in the development of today's computers and extrapolate information about the year 2335. As you saw in Figure 1.1, we plotted a linear regression line (line of best fit) for the number of transistors on a microprocessor. If we continue this line on the graph to the year 2335, we will find that the number of transistors on a microprocessor would be in the order of 3.3×10^{57} (this is 33 followed by 56 zeros or 3,300,000,000,000,000,000,000,000,000,000,000,000,000,000,000,000,000, 000,000). This is indeed a *lot* of transistors. From this mind-bogglingly large number it is not really possible to determine what the MIPS measurement of such a chip would be, so instead, extrapolating from existing processor MIPS, we have predicted that a chip of this size would be capable of processing 1.2×10^{48} MIPS. This is far more than the 6×10^7 MIPS necessary for Data's brain to function.

All this aside, one day, in the very near future, the ability for computer companies to produce smaller and smaller transistors will soon come to an end. Think of it like taking a piece of paper and halving it, then halving the half. How long can you continue to halve the object? Theoretically, you could halve the piece of paper until you reached the atomic level. Halving atoms then becomes a very scary business. Therefore, what happens when transistors become so small that they can no longer be made any smaller? Thomas Moore, himself, predicts the size of transistors will have reached their physical limitation by 2017. Applying the method of extrapolation with Moore's Law, we get approximately 387,710 MIPS as the processing limit for the year 2017. If processing speed advancement ends here, we fall very short of the 6×10^7 MIPS needed for Data's positronic brain. Therefore, a transistor-based brain is possibly out of the question for Data.

The solution to the restriction of transistors may lie in the basic unit of Data's brain. Whether it was foresight by Asimov in the naming of his futuristic electronic brain or not, the positron and its fellow atoms may hold the key to unlocking faster and faster processing speeds. Had Asimov coined the term *transistic* brain, instead of positronic brain, this discussion would have ended with the conclusion that the specifications of Data's brain are a physical impossibility. Nevertheless, as history has it, Asimov named the positronic brain after the positron discovered in 1932 by Carl D. Anderson, years before William Shockley invented the transistor in 1947.

Therefore, we must assume that Data's brain could not be constructed with today's technology. One ray of light found in the realm of science that strives to understand atomic particles, quantum mechanics, could help boost the processing capabilities of the humble transistor. Quantum mechanics applied in computer science is called quantum computing [Knill02].

Shockwave (*ENT#026*)

To explain how quantum computing works, we have to revisit the way in which computers store chunks of information using a bit. Recall that a bit can represent two values, a 1 or a 0. In quantum computing, the equivalent of a bit is called a quantum bit or *qubit*. In a traditional digital computer, a bit is defined by an electric charge between the plates in a capacitor. A charged capacitor represents a value of 1, and an uncharged capacitor represents 0. This means that the bit either has a value of 1 *or* a value of 0. In quantum computing, the capacitor is replaced with an atom. An atom can also represent 1 and 0 using distinct electric states; however, when prepared correctly, an atom can represent both 1 *and* 0 at the same time! When an atom is prepared to represent two states at the same time, it is in *coherent superposition*. This is a given concept in quantum mechanics[2]. The concept sounds a little strange, right? If the qubit represents both a 1 and a 0 at the same time, how are the states distinguished and processed? Furthermore, how does the qubit outperform the bit?

Let us have a look at an example. Consider a traditional byte of bits. In a byte we can store the numbers 00000000, 00000001, 00000011, 00000111, ... , 11111111. In all, that would be 256 separate values. A quantum byte made up of eight qubits can hold all 256 values *at the same time*. This means that any operation performed on the quantum byte is performed on all 256 values *at the same time* in a massive feat of parallel computing. To accomplish the same operation using the conventional byte the computer would have to perform the same operation on each of the 256 values separately. This would result in the computer having to perform 256 separate operations or using 256 processors in parallel. Therefore, the quantum computer can process just one byte of information 256 times faster than a conventional computer. However, it does not end there. The processing power of a quantum computer increases exponentially with the number of qubits being processed. That means a quantum computer can process $2^{\text{number of qubits}}$ values at any one time. Two quantum bytes could process 2^{16} or 65,536 values at once. Three quantum bytes could process 16,777,216 values at once, and so on.

So, where are all the quantum computers? Beside the obvious difficulties in working at an atomic level, the most critical problem occurs when information stored in the qubits dissipates into the surrounding environment. This is called *decoherence*. When you are working at the atomic level, all other components surrounding the qubits are also at the atomic level. Thus, physicists need to work out how the qubits can be contained and separated from their environment. Second, there is an issue of controlling the qubits. Physicists are able to observe quantum phenomena in atoms, but controlling them is a different issue. To date, quantum computers only exist in theory. The first steps toward building a real quantum computer will be in controlling the atoms and building simple transistor-like components with them. However, should they become a reality in the future, the exponential increase in processing power provided by these computers should be adequate for the development of Data's positronic brain. If we consider that in 2017 a conventional transistor-based computer will be able to process at around 387,710 MIPS, an equivalent quantum computer (replacing the transistors with atoms) will be able to process 2^{387710} MIPS. This, we assume, is a far larger number of MIPS than is needed by Data's positronic brain as our calculator refused to handle such a large number.

THRESHOLD (*VOY#139*)

So far we have established that the predicted processing power of future computers will be more than adequate for the processing speeds in Data's positronic brain. We now need to establish if the storage size of computer storage devices in the year 2335 will satisfactory hold 800 quadrillion bits. As storage, or *memory*, capacity in the computing domain is very rarely referred to in bits, we should convert this figure to bytes. Recalling that there are 8 bits in a byte, the storage capacity of Data's brain is 100 quadrillion bytes or 100 x 10^{15} bytes or 100 petrabytes. *Whoa! What on earth is a petrabyte?* This is a very good question. The use of the term byte preceded by a number of different prefixes has arisen as computing capacities has increased. Rather than referring to one thousand bytes, we say *kilobyte* (usually abbreviated as *kb*). Each successive prefix for the word *byte* refers to another thousand-fold of bytes. For example, one thousand kilobytes is referred to as a megabyte (*mb*), one thousand megabytes is referred to as a gigabyte (*gb*), one thousand gigabytes is a terabyte, one thousand terabytes is a petrabyte, one thousand petrabytes is an exabyte, one thousand exabytes is a zettabyte, and one thousand zettabytes is a yottabyte. If you have never heard of any of the terms after gigabyte, don't worry, you aren't alone. However, as computer memory capacity increases, these terms will become commonplace.

When we refer to a successive prefix being a thousand-fold of a previous one, we use the term *one thousand* quite loosely (as do most people). In the decimal system these prefixes refer to thousand-folds of numbers; for example, *kilo* stands for 1000. However, computers use a binary system and therefore a *kilo* is really 1024 (or 2^{10}). *Why?* Think back to when we demonstrated how to convert a binary number into a decimal number. The binary number for 1000 in decimal is 1111101000 binary. If each digit in the binary number requires one bit to represent it, then 1111101000 binary needs 10 bits. However, the largest number that can be represented in 10 bits is not 1111101000 but rather 1111111111 (when all the bits are set to 1). When 1111111111 binary is converted to decimal, the value is 1023. In computers there never seems to be enough storage space, so rather than rigidly sticking with the value of 1000 for a kilo and wasting the storage for another amount of 24, the extra space in the series of bits is used, allowing all bits to be set to a value of 1. This anomaly doesn't just occur in kilobytes but continues up the scale of bytes for all thousand-fold prefixes. Table 1.1 displays the real value of bytes in each thousand-fold.

TABLE 1.1   Correct byte values for each byte prefix

Term	Actual Bytes Value
kilobyte	1,024 bytes
megabyte	1,048,576 bytes
gigabyte	1,073,741,824 bytes
terabyte	1,099,511,627,776 bytes
petrabyte	1,125,899,906,842,624 bytes
exabyte	1,152,921,504,606,846,976 bytes
zettabyte	1,024 exabytes
yottabyte	1,024 zettabytes

Now that we know how many bytes of memory are needed by Data's positronic brain, all we need to do is extrapolate the size of future storage devices in the year 2335 using what we know about current storage device sizes. However, there are such a large array of computer storage devices that first we must determine what type would be best implemented in Data's brain. This is not to suggest that by 2335 we will not have come up with a new and improved method of data storage, but for now, contemporary devices are all we have to work with.

Charles Babbage proposed the first type of data storage for computers in 1822. Babbage, a student of the English Royal Astronomical Society[3], designed a steam-powered engine called a Difference Engine that used punched cards to store data. Some 120 years later, in the early 1940s, computer memory was created using vacuum tubes and resistors. Although electricity and vacuum tubes were a vast improvement on Babbage's steam engine, these computers still used punched cards for storage. The most significant advancement in computer memory came in 1966 with the invention of the first integrated circuit chip to store memory. It was created by Dr. Robert H. Dennard and functioned with just one transistor and a simple capacitor. In a PC this type of memory is called *random access memory*, or RAM for short. This is the computer's *main memory*. Most RAM is volatile. This means that data can only be stored in the chip while there is an electrical current running through it. Therefore, data can only be stored in RAM while the computer is running. When the computer is turned off the memory is erased.

Because of its volatile nature, RAM would be inappropriate for storing *Data's* 100 petabytes of data. In *TNG*: "Datalore" and *TNG*: "The Measure of a Man," Data is deactivated and then reactivated. Each time, he retains his memories, or what are commonly referred to as *memory engrams*. Recall the concept of the neural network and the way in which it models neurons and the pathways in the human brain. A collection of these connected neurons is used for storing a memory and is known as a memory engram. Data's memory engrams are stored on chips that can be added or removed from his positronic brain. This is demonstrated in *STIX*: *Insurrection*, when Geordie La Forge removes several engrams that are causing Data to behave erratically.

But we digress. At this point we are interested in examining the hardware required to achieve a *non-volatile* storage of Data's data. Contemporary storages devices such as the popular magnetic (hard disk drives and floppy disks) and optical (CD-ROMs) disks are currently capable of storing a mediocre number of gigabytes and are currently much too large to fit into a positronic brain. Therefore, we must look elsewhere for a solution, and a concept made popular by *Star Trek* culture may hold the key.

Take Me Out to the Holosuite (*DSN#554*)

In today's world, holograms are not solid (*VOY*: "Parallax"), are not capable of independent thought (*VOY*: "Tuvix"), are not programmed with over five million possible medical treatments (*VOY*: "Ex Post Facto"), do not release best selling operatic compact discs (*VOY*: "Virtuoso"), and cannot exceed their original programming (*VOY*: "Life Line"). In fact they cannot exist in our three dimensional environment. A hologram is purely a trickery of light, an image impregnated onto a flat surface that gives the illusion of three dimensions when viewed from different angles. Many examples exist in everyday life such as credit cards, magazine covers, and the little stickers on authentic Microsoft products. However, the characteristics of holograms have made them one of the latest research areas in data storage [Ashley00]. Magnetic and optical storage devices line up the 1s and 0s on a flat two dimensional surface. Because a holographic image has a depth of field, instead of storing one page of 1s and 0s, it can currently store many tens of terabytes per cubic centimeter. By viewing the hologram from different angles, we can view a different page of data. This means that 1 cubic centimeter of holographic storage can hold 125 gigabytes or 0.0001192 petrabytes. Under this model, we would need around 100 cubic centimeters to store Data's 100 petrabytes. This is roughly about the size of a Rubic's cube, maybe a little bigger. Given that the approximate volume of an average human brain is 1450 cubic centimeters, it is quite reasonable to assume this type of memory would be adequate for use in Data, depending on the size of the other components that make up a positronic brain.

INVASIVE PROCEDURES (*DSN#424*)

Assuming we have Data's physical brain, how might it be programmed? Data and Geordi often refer to something called Data's neural net. In AI today, we have a programming method called an artificial neural network. It is too much of a coincidence to think that this is not what the *Star Trek* writers are imagining as the foundation for Data's programming.

The inspiration for the artificial neural network structure comes from the very organ that provides us with our intelligence: the organic brain. The brain is made up of over 100 billion nerve cells called neurons. Neurons are found throughout the body's nervous system. They act as a medium through which the electrical and chemical signals that carry information throughout our bodies function. The neurons you will be most familiar with are the ones that exist in the peripheral nervous system and are bundled together to form nerves. These carry external signals to the brain. If you were to grab a bat'leth by the blade, the nerves in your partially severed fingers would relay information up the network of neurons in your arm to your spinal cord and then to your brain. This signal would tell your brain to take your hand off the sharp edge of the bat'leth before any more damage was done.

The typical neuron is composed of three parts: a cell body, an axon (with axon terminals), and dendrites. The dendrites receive signals from neighboring neurons and carry them to the cell body. The cell body transforms the signals and then passes them on to the axon, which relays the signal to the next neuron via the axon terminals. The neurons do not physically touch each other. They are separated by microscopically small gaps called *synapses*. The signal from one neuron to another hurtles across the gap in the form of an electrochemical substance called a neurotransmitter. Figure 1.3 illustrates the components of a neuron.

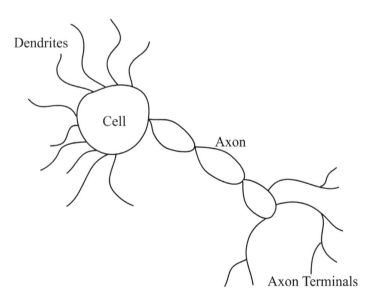

Dendrites

Cell

Axon

Axon Terminals

FIGURE 1.3   The basic structure of a neuron.

The whole process of message transmission through the network of neurons that is the nervous system is not all that dissimilar from electrical circuitry. Neurons are not always active and involved in message sending. In a resting state, a neuron is negatively charged on the inside and positively charged on the outside. The difference in the internal and external electrical charge of the neuron is called *polarization*. A neuron becomes excited or *activated* when it receives some kind of stimulation, either a message from a neighboring neuron or external sensations picked up by a sensory organ, such as the skin. At a particular point when the neuron is stimulated beyond its *threshold* the neuron becomes depolarized. Until a depolarized threshold value is reached nothing happens. Once depolarized, the neuron emits an electrical current or *spike discharge*. This electrical current moves down the axon and initiates the release of neurotransmitters that move across the synapse, and attach themselves to the dendrites of the receiving neuron, thus relaying the message. This electrochemical process for message relaying around a biological nervous system is the inspiration for the artificial neural network (ANN).

An ANN consists of nodes called *neurodes* or *artificial neurons* (more commonly just referred to as neurons), organized in a network. A single neuron has a number of inputs (x_1 to x_n) with associated weights (w_1 to w_n); a method for processing the input, N; and an output, y. An example of a basic neuron with two inputs is shown in Figure 1.4.

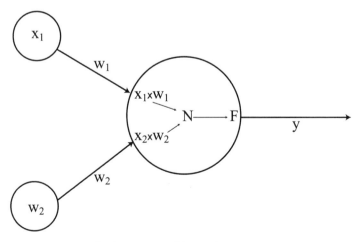

FIGURE 1.4 A single neuron with two inputs.

Before the neuron can process the input, each value of *x* is multiplied by its associated value of *w* and then added with the other input values.

The mathematics and programming involved in neural networks is a little complex; therefore, we won't explore it further at this stage. Suffice it to say, a neuron operates a little like they believe the neurons in the human brain work. The more a synaptic path is used, the more defined it becomes. For example, if you want to win at Kadis'kot (a board game played by Seven of Nine and Naomi Wildman in *VOY*: "Infinite Regress") you might try five different tactics. When one tactic works you receive what is known in psychology as positive reinforcement. When one of the tactics does not work, you receive negative reinforcement. Positive reinforcement strengthens the synaptic path between the neurons that represent the associated tactic. The stronger the synaptic path, the more often you will tend to use it. After a few tournaments of Kadis'kot you will have determined which of your chosen tactics works best.

The same premise is used in neural networks. The input to the network is processed into some kind of output. This output is assessed against some desired output and an error factor is calculated. This error factor is fed back into the neural network and used the next time it is fed input. In essence, it uses the error factor to make adjustments to the way it calculates the output.

Current-day neural networks are programmed with only one task in mind. It might be voice recognition, handwriting recognition, or navigating the surface of Mars. In *Star Trek*, Data's entire brain is referred to as a neural net for both the physical construction and processing sides. If Data's neural net is entirely physical, then all possible synaptic pathways would need to be created as physical connections at construction time. This would in essence disallow Data to form new synaptic pathways and would therefore drastically limit his abilities. However, we learn in *TNG*: "The Quality of Life" that the exocomps are able to create new synaptic pathways and, therefore, we might assume that Data can do so as well. These pathways would not be physical but somehow a programmatic process.

Even if this is the case, a neural network that could control all of Data's functionality would have to be massive, and it just might have to closely represent the some 100 billion neurons in the human brain more than we would like to think.

INQUISITION (*DSN#542*)

It seems that the idea of a positronic brain does not belong entirely in science fiction. Many current techniques and devices could be modified to develop the prototype of such an instrument. Like the computers of the past, it may initially turn out to be an enormous space-consuming machine. But without the initial computing prototypes we would not be where we are now. So, can we build a positronic brain by 2335? *Why of course!* Can we program it by then? With neural networks, maybe. *However, you'll have to read Part II to find out more!*

REFERENCES

[Ashley00] Ashley, J., Bernal, M.-P., Burr, G. W., Coufal, H., Guenther, H., Hoffnagle, J. A., M. Jefferson, C., Marcus, B., Macfarlane, R. M., Shelby, R. M. and Sincerbox, G. T., 2000, Holographic Data Storage, *IBM Journal of Research and Development, vol. 44*, no. 3.

[Knill02] Knill, E., Laflamme, R., Barnum, H., Dalvit, D., Dziarmaga, J., Gubernatis, J., Gurvits, L., Ortiz, G., Viola, L. and Zurek, W. H., "Introduction to Quantum Information Processing," in *Los Alamos Science*, Number 27, p2-37, (2002).

ENDNOTES

1. And two other prototypes of which B4 (*ST: Nemesis*) was one.
2. We have neither the room nor brain of Stephen Hawking to go into this here.
3. Surely perfect credentials for the earliest of Trekkers!!

CHAPTER 2

Physical Beings

CHAPTER OVERVIEW

In this chapter we will look at the feasibility of creating an android. A quick survey of your own body should tell you that creating an artificial being that not only has a human form but that also can physically operate like a human being is no easy feat. Just standing up requires a great deal of skill in balance, walking even more so. And what about stair climbing? Current-day androids are only just beginning to negotiate them. We will begin this chapter with an examination of the physical creation of Data the android and compare his specifications with a current-day android. From there we will move on to a quick overview of the computationally intensive methods used to control android movement.

BODY PARTS (*DSN#497*)

An android is a specialized robotic device artificially created to resemble a human being. The word *android* comes from the Greek *andr* meaning human and the suffix *eides* meaning *alike*. At the time of writing this book there are around 76 major android projects occurring worldwide. ASIMO is an android created by Honda Motor Company. It stands 1.2 meters tall, is 0.45 meters wide, 0.44 meters deep, and weighs 52 kgs. The technology with which ASIMO has been built enables it to stably walk two-legged on steps and slopes, to understand human gestures, and to move its head to follow a speaker. It is quite a remarkable device designed to *improve life in human society* [Honda03]. Though ASIMO doesn't quite stack up to the quality of Data, it is indeed an astounding achievement by today's technological standards. Table 2.1 displays ASIMO's technical specifications for comparison with Data.

TABLE 2.1   Data versus ASIMO

	Data	ASIMO
Dimensions	~175cm*	1.2m x 0.44m x 0.45m
Weight	> 37.7 kg**	52 kg
Control Unit	positronic brain	computer workstation

→

	Data	**ASIMO**
Sensors	sight, sound, touch, taste, smell	6-Axis foot area sensor, gyroscope, and acceleration sensor; sight, sound, touch (limited)
Power source	continuous recharging power cell***	38.4V/10AH Ni-MH battery
Max Walking Speed	fast****	1.6 km/h
Degrees of Freedom*****		
head	3	2
shoulder	3	3
elbow	1	1
wrist	3	1
fingers	1	1
hip	3	3
knee	1	1
ankle	3	2

* Given a 87.2 cm leg length (*STIIX: Insurrection*)

** Given 24.6 kg of tripolymer composites + 11.8 kgs of molybdenum-cobalt + 1.3 kgs of bioplast sheeting (*TNG*: "The Most Toys")

****STIIX: Insurrection*

**** In many episodes of *TNG*, Data is shown performing tasks at faster than human speed.

*****Degrees of Freedom is the term used to describe the range of movements of a joint. Data's range is comparable to a humans. DOF will be examined later in this chapter.

Other remarkable feets of android engineering include Tron X (shown in Figure 2.1), a 2.8 meter tall, 300 kg robot with over 200 pneumatic muscles [Gizmodo04] and HUBO, developed by the Korean Advanced Institute of Science and Technology, which unlike ASIMO can move its fingers independently. Another highly advanced form of android that has been built to resemble a human being is Kibertron, who stands 1.75 m tall and has 82 degrees of freedom. The difference between this android and the others mentioned is that Kibertron has been designed to be autonomous in that it is able to educate itself through its own motivation and purposes (much like Data does). There are many other android projects that we do not have the space to include here, but the interested reader is directed to *www.androidworld.com.*

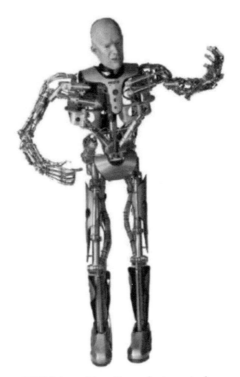

FIGURE 2.1   Tron-X, a robot created by German robotics company Festo.

© Festo. Reprinted with permission.

Basics (*VOY#142,146*)

To classify as a robot, a machine must have five main parts: a controller, an arm, a drive, an end effector, and a sensor. The controller of a robot is its brain. It acts to ensure that all other parts of the machine work together in unison. The robot's arm is the moveable part that does all the interacting with the physical world. Some robotic arms resemble human arms, but they usually come in all shapes and sizes, custom built for the task they are required to perform. In order to have the arm move, the robot is equipped with a drive. The drive is the engine which moves the joints of the arm. At the end of the arm is an end effector. This, in essence, is the robot's hand. It is crucial as it is the part of the robot that allows it to manipulate its environment. The hand can be any type of tool including tweezers, vacuum pumps, scissors, or simple gripping implements. In order to position the arm angle and the final location of the end effector, the robot requires sensors. The sensors act in the same way as our human ones of sight, sound, touch, taste, and smell. They allow the robot to detect its environment. Although most of today's working robots have limited sensor capability, they only need enough sensing abilities to complete their goals.

The first issue that you are faced with in attempting to get the robotic arm to move is creating a controller that can manipulate the joints of the arm to place the end effector in the right location. The theory behind such a controller is called inverse kinematics.

The Next Phase (*TNG#224*)

Although robots live in a 3D environment, it is best to begin a study of inverse kinematics in two dimensions. The simplest arm to manipulate with inverse kinematics is one with one joint. This simple structure also serves us well in examining the mathematics involved in more complex kinematics.

Given an elementary arm, the possible movement of the arm is in either a clockwise or anticlockwise direction about the joint, much like a hand on a clock. Given a target location, we want to adjust the orientation of the arm so the end effector is closest to that target. This is illustrated in Figure 2.2.

The analytical approach to solving this problem is to examine the initial orientation of the arm and the desired orientation of the arm. Having this information we can calculate the angle between the two orientations and apply this to the joint. In this case there is but one solution. What makes life more difficult is when more joints and arm parts are added. Figure 2.3 illustrates a two-jointed arm in two different positions, both which achieve the desired position of the end effector.

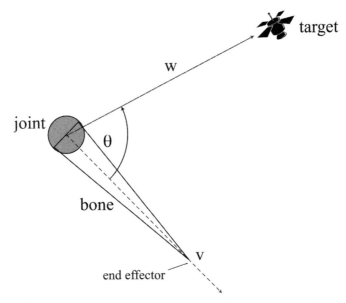

FIGURE 2.2   An elementary arm, end effector, and target.

To calculate the positions of the bones and joints, we can use the complex formulae derived in [Lander98]. We are giving the formulae in an attempt to illustrate the complexity of the task at hand. If you feel you have an appreciation for the process or don't desire the brain strain you can skip down to below Equation 2.3.

Before we begin, we should know the location of the first joint (the origin, O), the length of both arm parts (L_1 and L_2) and the target location (T_2). What we need to determine is the location of the second joint (T_1), and the amount to turn each joint through (θ_1 and θ_2). We can find θ_2 using the length of the arm parts and the final position of the end effector (T_2). The formula is shown as Equation 2.1.

$$\theta_2 = \arccos\left(\frac{Tx_2^2 + Ty_2^2 - L_1^2 - L_2^2}{2\,L_1 L_2}\right) \quad (2.1)$$

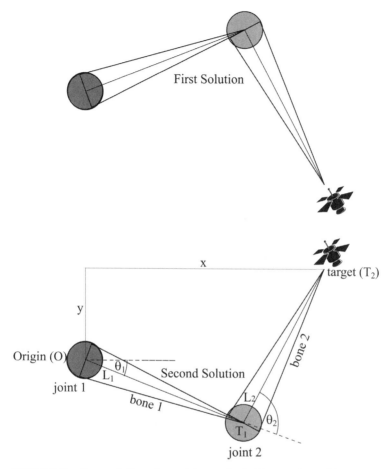

FIGURE 2.3 Two solutions for solving a single kinematic problem.

Once this has been found, θ_1 can be calculated using Equation 2.2.

$$\theta_1 = \arctan\left(\frac{y(L_2\cos(\theta_2) + L_1) - x(L_2\sin(\theta_2))}{x(L_2\cos(\theta_2) + L_1) - y(L_2\sin(\theta_2))} \right) \qquad (2.2)$$

Finally, the location of T_1 can be determined by Equation 2.3.

$$T_1 = \left(L_1\cos(\theta_1), L_2\sin(\theta_1) \right) \qquad (2.3)$$

Bear in mind, these equations are for models with just two joints and two arm parts. The solution is known as a closed form as it cannot be applied to other models. It can calculate the exact location of the arm parts very quickly. As these equations are restricted to a two joint model, as more joints are added, new formulae need to be derived to handle the models. As the number of joints increases the solutions becomes increasingly complex and often there can be an infinite number of solutions. For example, a six-jointed model has about $\propto^{18}$ solutions.

As you can imagine, this type of analytical approach is less than desirable as it could be impossible to come up with a decent solution. This brings us to an iterative solution where each angle is adjusted slightly through a loop of iterations until the desired solution, if there is one, is found. We have probably floored you with Equations 2.1 through 2.3 and therefore will not go into this algorithm here. The interested reader is directed to read [Lander98].

TIN MAN (*TNG#168*)

Degree of Freedom (DOF) is another important aspect in moving skeletal structures such as robotic arms, because many of the joints in a skeleton have restrictions on how they can be manipulated. The DOF of a joint defines how many axes the joint can rotate around. For example, the human elbow has one DOF because it can only bend in one direction. We examined the DOFs for Data in Table 2.1. Along with this restriction the elbow also has a limit of rotation from zero to about 175 degrees. This would be the total of the movement made if you stretched your arm out straight and then touched your hand to your shoulder. The human neck has 3 DOF. You can experience this by 1) nodding as though you are saying *yes*; 2) shaking your head from side to side as though you are saying *no*; and 3) tilting your head back and forth as if you are trying to touch your ears to your shoulders. Each of these DOFs also has a different set of rotation restrictions. For example, if we assume zero degrees to be looking straight ahead, then the second DOF (saying 'no') has a range of $+90^0$ to -90^0 depending on how flexible you are. A robot such as Data that looks and moves like a human would have to have these restrictions placed on his joint structure.

PROJECTIONS (*VOY#117*)

In this chapter we have examined some methods for creating a subsection of moving android parts and the mathematics behind controlling these types of limbs. The physical creation of a fully functioning android requires a massive effort; however, if you are interested in building your own android head, check out *howtoandroid.com/HowToBuildRobotHead.html*.

Androids are no longer robotic machines belonging to the future. They are indeed a current-day reality. However, as we have seen in this chapter, although the technology exists and may soon exist to create a being of Data's sophistication, there is still a lot of work to do. It seems that the physical embodiment of the android is far closer to being realized than the programming of its positronic brain.

REFERENCES

[Gizmodo04] Gizmodo, 2004, Festo's Humanoid Robot, Gawker Media, available *http://www.gizmodo.com/archives/festos-humanoid-robot-015276.php* March 2005.

[Honda03] Honda Motor Co. 2003, ASIMO Technical Information, American Honda Motor Co., Inc., Corporate Affairs & Communications.

[Lander98] Lander, J., "Making Kine More Flexible," Game Developer Magazine (November 1998): pp15–22.

CHAPTER 3

Holographic Beings

CHAPTER OVERVIEW

The EMH is not restricted by the same physical attributes that Data possesses. Being a robotic device, Data is restricted by the nature of his body and the components of his positronic brain. The EMH has no such physical restrictions; he could easily look like a Klingon Targ should he so wish. In fact, in *VOY*: "Blink of an Eye," the EMH is able to change his appearance to blend in with an alien culture. The limitations of the EMH are his needs to be in the vicinity of a holographic projector and to have hardware to run his program. When on *Voyager*, the EMH has to rely on the processing capabilities of *Voyager's* computer core. We also know that the EMH has dedicated space on the ship's systems; in *VOY*: "Virtuoso," he is informed by B'lanna that he can have his singing subroutines extended but at the price of deleting some of his medical database.

In this chapter we contemplate the existence of *virtual* artificial beings such as the EMH and the multitude of Holodeck characters littered among various episodes of *TNG*, *VOY*, and *DSN*. When Wil Riker steps onto a Holodeck for the first time in *TNG*: "Encounter at Farpoint," he is astonished by its complexity and the authenticity of the projected images. As you will discover, we too can be amazed at the three dimensional photographic accuracy of today's holograms, but is our scientific understanding advanced enough to one day make them into living artificial beings?

We begin by discussing the science behind holograms as we know them today and contemplate whether we can expect to one day have our very own Holosuites.

HOLLOW PURSUITS (*TNG#169*)

Do you remember seeing your first hologram? Maybe it was an image of a dove on a VISA card or the Microsoft logo on a Microsoft product authentication sticker. Whatever it was, it was surely a far cry from the holographic technology of the 24th century, the type of technology used to generate the characters on the Holodeck, create three dimensional projections in the *Enterprise-D's* briefing room, and, most importantly, give Emergency Medical Holograms substance. What you may not have known is that holograms aren't really anything new and existed long before Microsoft stickers.

The word *hologram* originates from the Greek and, when translated, means *complete message[1]*. A hologram itself is a complete visual representation of the exact size and three dimensionality of an object using an immaterial light field. The scientist who invented the hologram in 1947, Dr Dennis Gabor, won the Nobel Peace Price in physics for his theory. While a hologram is an image, it is obviously different from other everyday images. The principal that sets holograms apart is *interference*. Traditional images taken by a camera work by capturing the light reflected by an object using a focused lens, whereas a hologram captures the object's reflected light combined with an additional light shone directly onto the capturing medium. The other difference between ordinary images and holograms is that ordinary images can be created using white light (the light you get from the sun, light bulb, or camera flash), whereas holograms are created using lasers. The reason lasers are used comes back to the basic principle of interference.

In order to understand the notion of interference, we first need to understand the nature of light. Light is a series of electromagnetic waves propagating through space[2] with differing wavelengths and vibrations. These waves contain light particles called photons. Photons are the result of energy being release by electrons. In short, atoms contain electrons that orbit the atom's nucleus at certain distances. When an atom receives an energy boost (through a chemical or electrical interaction) the electrons can move into higher, or excited, orbits. This makes the atom somewhat unstable, and in order to return to a resting state the electrons must return to their usual orbits. To do this, they need to release some energy. The resulting energy release is a photon.

To visualize light waves, imagine ocean waves. Their up and down movement on the surface is what we refer to as the vibration, and the distance between one crest and another is the wavelength. Just as ocean waves have different wavelengths and vibrations, so to do light waves. It is the wavelength of a light wave that determines its color. For example, red light has a shorter wavelength than blue light. What we refer to as white light is in fact a conglomeration of all the colors of light being viewed at the same time. In essence, the light waves interfere with each other and are added together to produce a single light wave perceived by the human eye as white. An excellent way to see this result is to cross the light from red, green, and blue light sources, as shown in Figure 3.1. When the three lights are combined they produce white light. Note other colors are also formed where only two of the primary colors are combined.

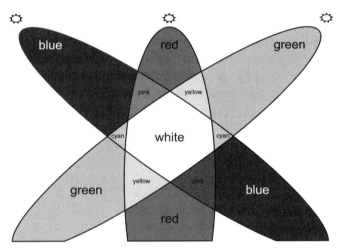

FIGURE 3.1   White light is a result of combining red, green, and blue lights.

Unlike mixing different colored paints, where it would be nearly impossible to separate the colors, white light can be separated. Figure 3.2 (a) shows the effect of passing white light through a glass prism. The longer the wavelength the more the light wave is diffracted[3] when it passes from the glass to the air. Blue light is diffracted the most[4].

What does all this have to do with laser light and coherence? If you have ever seen a laser light you will know they are most often red. Figure 3.2 (b) illustrates that red light (and any other single color for that matter) does not separate into other colors as it passes through a prism. Therefore it is concluded that a single color is made up of waves with the same wavelength. With normal light however, the waves do not move in unison. So

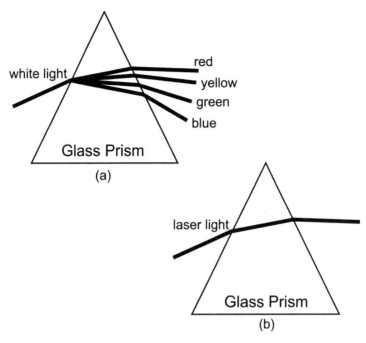

FIGURE 3.2 White light being diffracted through a prism. (a) White light being passed through a prism separates the pure component colors. (b) Laser light is pure and therefore is not separated by a prism.

although they are all the same size, they are not in phase, as shown in Figure 3.3 (a). When the waves are in phase, we say they are *coherent*, and this is the very nature of laser light as shown in Figure 3.3 (b).

Now that you understand the nature of light, or at the very least have a better idea of what we are talking about, we can get back to the creation of a hologram.

A hologram is created using the interference of light waves. As we have previously seen, white light already has an interference pattern; however, we do not have control over that interference. Because laser light is coherent, if the phases of two lasers differ we can measure the interference and make better use of it. The setup for creating a hologram involves the splitting of a

red light

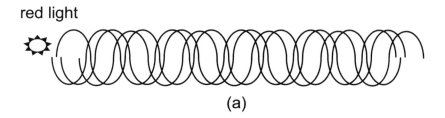

(a)

red laser light

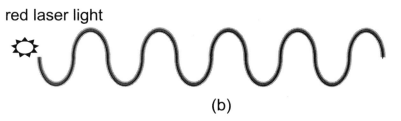

(b)

FIGURE 3.3 Incoherent and coherent light waves. (a) Incoherent light waves are out of phase. (b) Coherent light waves are in phase.

laser beam into two parts, shown in Figure 3.4. One part shines directly onto a holographic plate (the recording file) and the other part bounces off the subject and onto the plate. When the two split beams reunite on the medium, they cause an interference pattern between the original beam and the one that has interacted with the subject. To visualize this interference pattern, imagine throwing two rocks into a pond at the same time a couple of meters apart. Each splash location creates neat ripples centered around the impact. When the ripples finally spread out enough, they will come into contact with each other. This is an interference pattern. After the pattern is recorded on the holographic plate, the plate is processed and a hologram is born.

An interesting fact about holograms, and one that has absolutely nothing to do with *Star Trek*, is that the whole image is recorded on every part of the plate. What this means is if part of the final hologram's plate is cut off, the whole image remains. Unlike a traditional paper photograph where, if you cut off someone's head, you can't see the head in the photograph anymore, if you cut off a hologram's head you would end up with two copies of the entire hologram.

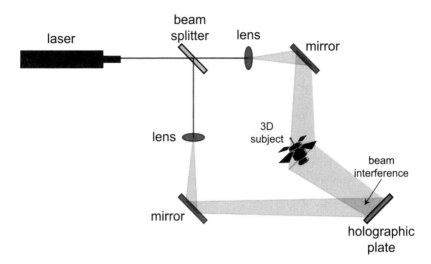

laser

beam splitter

lens

mirror

lens

3D subject

beam interference

mirror

holographic plate

FIGURE 3.4 Laser setup for hologram creation.

Now obviously the EMH is not the type of hologram we know today. In *VOY*: "The Phage," an altercation between Lieutenant Tom Paris and the EMH reveals his true nature. When Neelix experiences the unsolicited removal of his lungs by a race called the Vidians, the EMH comes up with the idea of creating for Neelix a set of holographic lungs by modifying his own holographic emitter array. Paris refutes the doctor's idea stating that a hologram is simply a projection of light held within a magnetic containment field and that there is no real matter involved. The EMH responds to Paris' insight by slapping Paris across the face, illustrating that by modulating his magnetic containment field, the EMH can allow matter to interact with his body or pass straight through.

Holograms as we know them are virtual. They don't really exist in the form we perceive them, but are contained on a medium such as a plastic or glass plate. Thus they have a solid component. One type of hologram that is perceived as being separated from its medium is a *real* hologram. A real hologram appears to sit in front of the plate and is thus viewed as being in the real world, as opposed to a *virtual* hologram, which appears on the opposite site of the plate like an image in a mirror. The point is, you could pass your hand right through a real hologram because you wouldn't need to come into contact with the plate. Unfortunately, there is no way a hologram can have any solid component other than its plate (and possibly the light source being used to view it).

The *Star Trek* idea of a hologram (especially in the case of the EMH) is a solid/transparent entity created through the magnetic manipulation and containment of a projection of light from an external source (emitter). We could liken it to shining a torch into a room and expecting the light to be captured by some invisible force and molded to represent something real. An interesting idea; however, there are a few problems.

First of all, can magnets affect light? The short answer is *no*. Shine a torch through a magnetic field and nothing will happen. For the reason, we again need to look at things from the atomic level. We know magnetic fields can influence some things and even some things involving light. A fantastic example is that of the northern or southern lights (Aurora Borealis and Aurora Australis). The auroras are produced when solar waves from the sun get caught in the earth's magnetic field and come into contact with the gases of the earth's ionosphere (60 to 600 km above the surface). The sun's solar winds are clouds of highly charged particles called ions. Such a cloud is known as plasma[5].

Magnetic containment fields can be used to control the flow of very hot plasma such as that in nuclear fusion reactors. Because of the extremely high temperatures needed for nuclear fusion, magnetic fields are used to keep the plasma out of contact with the walls of the container, which would otherwise melt.

You may conclude from these examples that a magnetic field can trap light, but alas, it is not the case. The photons released by the plasma are what we see as light. Photons have no charge; they are inert[6]. Only charged particles can be manipulated by a magnetic field.

It might be possible to create an EMH if the holographic emitter produced ions instead of photons and the magnetic containment field was used to keep the ions in place. Of course, sickbay would then have to be filled with some kind of gas that would interact with the ions to release the photons. Remember, though, from our previous discussion, the release of a photon means an ion is returning to a less charged state, and therefore we would need a ready supply of ions continuously being produced by the emitter. This might explain why the EMH (before he procured his mobile emitter) could not leave the confines of sickbay. It would not be enough just to move the magnetic containment field, because once the photonic emissions from the existing ions faded, so too would the image of the doctor. This is all beside the fact that we would also have to control the colors of the photons and produce an extremely detailed and mailable magnetic field.

Another possibility would be to have the EMH's appearance projected into the room in the same way a movie projector projects an image onto a wall. This, however, would make the EMH two dimensional and incapable of holding medical instruments. If we could create a three dimensional projection, the program recreating the EMH's physical appearance would have to be quite advanced. First, the EMH would be the projection of an animation. This animation would have to run at similar speeds to a movie to be convincing. This is somewhere in the vicinity of 25 frames/second, a far smaller amount than the 100 frames we expect Data to be able to perceive as we discover in Chapter 4. Second, the animation of the EMH would have to be dynamic. This means that you could not preprogram the appearance and actions of the EMH, because you don't know exactly what he might be required to do. It might be possible to preproduce a number of canned action sequences and reuse them, but after a while the EMH would become very predictable. If the program were to calculate the next posture or action of the EMH, it would need to perform complex calculations like the ones we examined on kinematics in Chapter 2. Last but not least, the animation would have to be in real time. Any program producing the animation would have to be able to determine what the next frame looks like and process it fast enough to redraw 25 of them every second. While this is not an impossible task, with today's technology the level of detail in the EMH would be a struggle. However, as processing power increases, a projection of an animation is a more likely way to go.

VIRTUOSO (*VOY#234*)

Some technology that exists today does in fact combine animated projections with holographic plating to create holograms like the ones you see projected in the *Enterprise-D* briefing room or the miniature replications of the doctor that he gives out to his fans in *VOY*: "Virtuoso." Unfortunately, these are not solid or interactive: true solid holograms of the form taken by the EMH or characters on the Holodeck are a present day scientific impossibility. However, we also used to believe the world was flat!

ENDNOTES

1. A fitting description given the EMH's use as a long distance carrier pigeon in VOY: "Message in a Bottle."
2. We don't use space in this instance to mean a vacuum but simply a distance between a light source and a viewer.
3. The term used to describe how light is bent when it passes from one medium density to another. This illusion can be observed when looking at things below water from above. The objects appear bigger and also to be in a slightly different location from where they actually are.
4. The very reason the sky is blue!
5. Yes, the same stuff that powers the warp core.
6. So much for the photonic cannon! (*VOY*: "Tinker, Tenor, Doctor, Spy").

CHAPTER 4

Sensing the Environment

CHAPTER OVERVIEW

Machines such as Data and other artificial beings in *Star Trek* do not seem
limited by a lack of sensors. Even Honda's ASIMO has a good fundamental
set of sensors. The difference between Data's and ASIMO's sensors is the
level of sophistication. For example, when Data hears something, he is able
to fully comprehend it, whereas ASIMO simply knows that he heard a sound.
This is not a limitation of ASIMO's hearing sensor but rather of the software
that interprets the sounds. Humans have five sensors that they can use to
sense their environment. To create a machine with the same level of sophistication for operating in the same environment that we do, the machine
must also have these sensors. The following sections look at each of the
human sensors and how they are starting to be included in robotic devices.

SECOND SIGHT (*DSN#429*)

Human eyes detect visual objects with two types of nerves located on the
retina used for capturing visual data: cones and rods. Cones are used primarily for detecting colors, and rods detect shades and movement. Having
two eyes also means that we can see things stereoscopically, or in three dimensions. This allows us to perceive depth and separate objects in the environment from one another.

Robotic sight is better known as machine vision. As a research domain,
machine vision is over 20 years old. Some applications that fit into this
realm are bar code scanners, digital video cameras, and motion detectors.
To build an android such as Data that not only takes a photographic representation of his environment but can actually understand what it is looking at is quite another thing.

Humans process visual information at approximately 100 frames per
second. This is much faster than the average digital video camera, which
captures about 30 frames per second. Each frame captured by the eye is
processed for luminance, color, and motion. Performing this action with
today's computers is extremely complex and requires an awful lot of processing power. As computer power increases in the future, this action can
only improve. This limitation aside, computer programs are becoming
quite adept at processing what they do see. Machine vision is currently

used in applications such as packaging, sorting tasks, navigation, medical diagnosis, playing games, and facial recognition systems.

Biological vision is a difficult act to follow. Of course, depending on the type of task the machine vision is needed for, it need not be as precise or limited. Table 4.1 lists the major functions of the human eye and compares them with current machine vision technologies. Note that in this table we include the eye-brain as a functioning pair, because machine vision requires not only image capture but a computer for the processing.

TABLE 4.1   Human eye-brain functions verse machine vision*

Function	Human Eye-Brain	Machine Vision
Spatial Resolution	Excellent, non-linear	Poor, linear
Gray-Scale Resolution	Limited	4000 shades or more
Gray-Scale Dynamic Range	Excellent, non-linear	Limited, typically linear
Color Resolution	Limited—(128 hues, 28 saturations)	Millions of colors
Complex Color	Excellent	Poor
Three Dimensional Perception	Powerful but poor measurement precision	Complex and precise
Learning	Learns by example	Programmed
Processing of simple and defined tasks	Slow	Very fast
Processing of complex and ambiguous tasks	Very fast	Very slow
Sensitive to Illumination	No	Yes
Processing	Massively parallel, highly non-linear and intuitive	Serial, logic, usually linear and fixed

* Adapted from [Novini98]

As we have already established that Data's brain processing capacity of 6×10^7 MIPS is a real possibility in the future, we can speculate about his ability to process sight like a human. To begin, Data has two eyes. This is extremely important if Data is going to view the world stereoscopically. The differing viewpoints of the eye cameras allow for a kind of triangulation that creates a field of depth. If you are familiar with the color settings on your computer screen you know that you can set it to display some 16 million colors. In reality though, the human eye can only detect 128 pure colors (called hues). In addition it can also detect 28 saturations of these colors. The saturation of colors is how much white is mixed into the color. In total, this would make $128 \times 28 = 3584$ colors. Unlike our eyes, when a digital device takes an image it registers it as a rectangle consisting of many individual dots of color called pixels. To determine the number of pixels Data's eyes might capture of a view, we must look at the resolution of the human eye.

Let's work with a simple example of a view directly in front of the eye that is 90 degrees by 90 degrees, similar to looking out of a window. The number of pixels in this image would be 324,000,000 pixels (according to [Clark05]). However, the human eye moves around to take in more detail of a scene and actually sees a field of view of around 120 degrees[1]. This would equate to 576,000,000 pixels. Because this is just one snap-shot, or frame, in our viewing, we then need to multiply this by the 100 frames per second that would need to be processed. Therefore, we could assume that for Data to process images in the same way that we do, he would need to process 576 gigapixels/second.

The color value of each of these pixels would be represented by binary code. Because we have already established that there are 3584 colors that each pixel could be, we would need 12 bits to store this as a binary code. Therefore 576 gigapixels/second x 12 bits/pixel would require processing of 6912 gigabits/second, which is about 805 gigabytes/second and which is indeed within Data's processing capabilities.

Of course Data must be capable of not only the capture of the pixels but also of realtime processing and understanding of the image. As you can see in Table 4.1, machine vision at the current time is very slow in processing complex and ambiguous images. For most visual recognition tasks, current-day computers are programmed with pattern matching algorithms. One of the most well known applications of these algorithms is for facial recognition. The program learns from images of people and then goes about trying to match a new image against the database. It does not take a genius of disguise to put on a wig and glasses to fool the system. Another system developed by IBM called VeggieVision that uses visual recognition distinguishes between different types of vegetables and fruits. It is efficient at differentiating apples from oranges but is less successful at telling different orange varieties apart.

From this we can conclude that visual data capture of the type implemented in Data is not impossible. While current day processing of such images is less than perfect, especially in real world scenarios, as processing speeds increase and we learn more about the way the human brain processes vision, it is indeed a possibility that Data might have visual abilities comparable with humans.

AS LOUD AS A WHISPER (*TNG#132*)

There are essentially two areas developing sound sensing capabilities in robotic devices. These include the most well known, speech recognition, and a more general area focused on auditory environments, sound recognition. We will begin our discussion here by examining the former.

Speech recognition is the process whereby a computer program converts spoken speech into data that it can then process. The speech is captured in its analog form by a microphone and converted into a digital signal. This signal is then analyzed by the computer and an estimate of the original speech in words is generated. For the human brain this type of conversion is a snap, but for the computer it is a monumental task. At the beginning of the 1990s the best programs were getting a 15% error rate given 20,000 words. While this has dropped in some instances to around 2%, it can still greatly vary between speakers [Matthews02]. The program has to accommodate different languages, accents, the speaker's age, the speaker's gender, and different words that sound the same.

In brief, speech recognition works by splitting speech up into linguistic units called phonemes. For example, *ao* is the phoneme for the pronunciation of the *o* in *dog*. There are about 40 phonemes in the half a million words of the English language. Speech recognition works by taking the sound wave of the speech and running it through a mathematical analysis called a Fourier Transformation. Without getting too technical, this transformation pulls out the phonemes. Once the phonemes have been identified they need to be converted into words. The most common method for doing this is called a Markov Model. We will look closer at the details of a Markov Model in Chapter 5, when we examine speech generation. In essence, the model stores a complex chain of phonemes in which one phoneme is connected to another along with the probability that the later phoneme follows the previous one in speech. These probabilities are used by the program to determine the most likely word that was spoken from the phonemes it perceived.

Although speech recognition has been at the forefront of sound processing for some time, there are also many other sounds in the environment that are just as important for an artificial being to be able to identify. The general field of sound recognition examines these. The same type of sound wave analysis used with speech can be performed in attempting to recognize environmental sounds other than spoken words, such as jangling keys, footsteps, breaking glass, and twigs snapping. Models that use basic word elements such as phonemes are not appropriate for analyzing these sounds in order to classify what they are, because they do not have phoneme components. This makes the Markov Model inappropriate. However, there are many other methods that can be used. The one identified as being quite appropriate is called Learning Vector Quantization (LVQ) [Cowling02]. In brief, LVQ is a competitive learning method that takes data and attempts to find structure by dividing the data into clusters using straight lines. At the beginning a computer program using this method can be instructed by a person regarding what the sounds it is hearing are. It can then take future sounds and analyze them to see which cluster they fall into. The program can then make an educated guess as to what the sound it heard was.

Although LVQ is efficient at recognizing environmental sounds, it isn't as good as other techniques in recognizing speech. We could conclude from this that if an android such as Data were developed with the sense of hearing, it would have to include different programs to process and recognize different sounds. As an alternative, a more universal approach to sound processing would have to be discovered.

In the Flesh (*VOY#198*)

In *STIIX: First Contact*, there is a scene where Picard and Data are on Earth examining the *Phoenix* rocket, which was instrumental in humanity's first contact with extraterrestrials. Picard, while examining the *Phoenix*, tells Data that touch can connect you to an object in a very personal way, making the object more real. In response to this, Data places his hand on the rocket, apparently analyzing the surface. He notes imperfections in the titanium casing and temperature variations in the fuel manifold. He concludes that the rocket is no more real to him than it was before. However, although Data knew what the *Phoenix* was already, he now had extra information about it that was not available by merely looking at it.

The scientific field devoted to developing a sense of touch in machines is called robotic haptics. This domain explores the way in which robotic effectors can sense the nature of the things that they come into contact with. In order for a robotic device to feel an object, it must exhibit precise control and dexterity. Haptic robots already exist. They are used for feeling their way around objects in order to create a 3D virtual representation of the object in a computer. These types of robots limit the amount of information they sense based on the requirements of the model. For example, if a virtual representation were needed to represent the general shape of an object, the surface texture might be ignored.

In *STIIX: First Contact* Data receives the gift of experiencing real human touch from the Borg Queen. After he is captured, the Borg installed a layer of skin (complete with pores and hair) onto his wrist. He asks if they are using a polymer-based neural relay to transmit organic nerve impulses to the central processor of his positronic net. The Borg Queen insists he talks too much. While trying to escape, Data is slashed across the newly installed flesh, which halts his attempt to flee. Instead, he nurses his wrist, perplexed by the pain. Obviously this level of feeling touch could be quite debilitating for a robotic device.

Fortunately, for a machine such as Data, the possibility of restricting the haptic sense would be quite a conscious one, enabling him to choose the level of detail with which he feels. If he is attempting to negotiate some unknown complex terrain (possibly in the dark), his senses need to be heightened and he needs to know what he is touching, how to touch it, and how to respond. In addition, tactile knowledge of the environment can provide a more complete view of the world for characteristics that can not be sensed by other means. For example, if a surface is extremely hot, it might not be evident by sight or smell. Being able to feel heat could be a limb-saving essential if walking backwards into lava.

At the time of writing this book, the autonomous exploration of an environment using touch is a research field in its infancy. What needs to be considered are the movements of the robot's effectors (which might be robotic fingers), the fragility of the object being touched, and the movement of the effectors around the object.

A Taste of Armageddon (*TOS#023*)

In *STVII: Generations*, Data is capable of taste. Having had his emotion chip installed, Geordi takes him to Ten Forward where he tries a new drink provided by Guinan. Data's taste sensors determine the drink to be foul tasting, which in turn triggers an emotional reaction (more about this in Part III).

You may not have considered machines being able to smell and taste and might think it is something best left for science fiction, but they already exist. In the same way that insects use pheromone trials to communicate, a robotic device can be equipped with a quartz crystal microbalance (QCM) sensor to follow chemical trails. These types of robots are useful in detecting gas and chemical leaks, food spoilage, water pollutants, and diagnosing health issues [SpaceDaily04].

E-Nose, being developed by NASA, has 32 small sensors which are collectively the size of a human nose. The sensors are connected to a computer that registers data and attempts to identify smells. E-Nose is being developed to identify organic and non-organic particles in the air inside the space shuttle. It will act as an early warning system for astronauts if their air becomes contaminated.

The data collected by smell sensors has to be analyzed just as the data collected from the sensors discussed in the previous sections. Basically the process needs to pattern match the incoming data with smell data it has already accumulated and identified. This process can be performed by a neural network, LVQ or any other pattern recognition AI technique.

PERSISTENCE OF VISION (*VOY#124*)

As a last word on robotic sensors—because humans have limited capabilities, it is not beyond a machine to improve on them. For example, humans only see a very limited range of light waves. There is no reason why a medical android could not be equipped with x-ray vision for patient diagnosis. By providing androids with sensors that are superior to those of humans, the androids could become valuable tools, able to go where humans cannot and to detect trouble in the environment that is beyond our own sensing.

REFERENCES

[Clark05] Clark, R. N., 2005, "Notes on the Resolution and Other Details of the Human Eye, Roger N. Clark, available *http://clarkvision.com/imagedetail/eye-resolution.html*, June 2005.

[Cowling02] Cowling, M., Sitte, R., 2002. "Analysis of Speech Recognition Techniques for Use in a Non-Speech Sound Recognition System." In *Proceedings of DSPCS 2002*, Manly, Australia.

[Novini98] Novini, A., 1998, "Future Trends in Machine Vision", Applied Vision Company, available *http://www.appliedvision.com/presenta.htm*, June 2005.

[SpaceDaily04] Space Daily, "The 'Nose' Knows A Sweet Smell Of Success", available *http://www.spacedaily.com/news/robot-04zc.html*, April 2005.

ENDNOTES

1. This is being very conservative.

PART II

Mind

CHAPTER 5

Presence of Mind

CHAPTER OVERVIEW

Although the hardware that the EMH and Data rely on is somewhat different, at their very core must run a basic program. It is on top of this program that all of their other subroutines and databases are created. In this chapter we will examine the underlying structure of the systems that run on today's computers. We envisage that any such programs running on the hardware of an artificial being would not be that much different.

We begin by examining computer operating systems, their organisation and purpose. This is followed by some examples of how such systems would perform in Data and the EMH.

I DON'T HAVE A LIFE, I HAVE A PROGRAM[1]

A program to a computer is what consciousness is to an organic being. It controls and instructs the computer. Most computers have a kind of master program or operating system. This is a program that runs continuously on the computer and takes care of internal monitoring (for example, the time), maintains peripheral connections (links with the outside world), performs utility functions (running the screen saver), and carries out error checking (for example, "Is the hard drive accessible?"). Microsoft Windows, Mac OS X, and Linux are operating systems. Most operating systems come with a number of complementary programs that help any operator access and use the computer. Programs are simply a set of instructions for the computer to follow in order to achieve a specific task. In addition to the operating system programs, other programs can also be written and added to enhance the performance of the computer.

The key to the operating system is that it runs continuously (until you turn the computer off). A lot of programs just run through a set of instructions and then end. If the operating system did this, the computer would turn on, check its internal settings, and then shut down. This would be pretty useless. So after performing all the preliminary tasks, the operating system just sits back and monitors what is going on. All operating systems do this.

The basic outline of an operating system's processing is shown in Figure 5.1. Here the processing begins with the initialization. This is the step previously mentioned, where the operating system is first turned on and the preliminary check is performed. Resource allocation also occurs at this point. For example, the amount of memory needed by the operating system can be allocated.

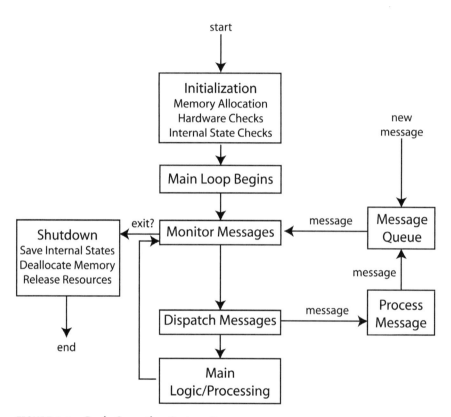

FIGURE 5.1   Basic Operating System Processes.

The operating system must not only perform system checks, it must also provide the computer with some basic functions. For example, it contains instructions in the form of smaller dedicated programs that tell the computer how to write data to a floppy disk or how to operate a modem.

It also contains a set of subroutines that take care of user interactions. For example, when you hit a key on a laptop, the letter on the key appears in the word processor. This doesn't happen by magic. Usually this type of functionality is built into the word processing program itself, but it works on the same premise as the operating system. Previously we said that the operating system runs continuously, monitoring the computer. This is shown in Figure 5.1 as the *main loop*. What it is monitoring are the occurrences of certain messages. Whenever you kit a key, move the mouse, or speak into the microphone, a message depicting these incoming actions is placed in a *message queue*. The operating system removes the message from the queue and processes it as specified by higher level programs (if appropriate). For example, the operating system can detect the pressing of a key but unless it has instructions on what do to with that key it will do nothing. If a word processor program is running, it will have registered a particular subroutine with the operating system that allows the key press event to type the appropriate character into the document.

There are all types of events that occur when a computer is running. Most of these are captured by the operating system. Even the startup of a program is an event. The EMH has an event executed when a crew member enters sickbay and says, "Computer. Activate the Emergency Medical Hologram." The startup routine of the EMH always has the EMH announcement, "State the nature of the medical emergency." In *VOY*: "The Cloud," the EMH and Lieutenant B'lanna Torres discuss changing the greeting to something that resembles a better bedside manner[2].

This form of operating is called *event driven* processing. Basically, the operating system sits around and waits for an event to occur. When an event does occur (key pressed, mouse moved, patient enters sick bay, etc.) a message is placed in the message queue. If the operating system has appropriate message processing instructions as to what to do with the message, it acts on it; otherwise the process moves to the *main logic/processing* part of the *main loop*. This part of the operating system process handles the majority of the operations. It will include all processing that must occur within the OS that is not handled by message processing. This would include all operations that should occur regardless of any interaction with the computer. As these operations occur within the *main loop*, they will happen each time the loop goes around, which for the operating system is continual until the computer is shut down. If the process of saying, "State the nature of the medical emergency" was placed in the *main logic* area of the EMH, the EMH would persistently repeat this line over and over again until it was deactivated.

A more appropriate process that could occur in the *main logic* would be the monitoring of the EMH's states. For example, the main logic of the EMH could prevent it from bumping into objects by continually monitoring its distance to other surrounding objects and adjusting the EMH's movements accordingly. If for some reason the EMH did collide with another object, this collision would cause an event message to be placed in the message queue to be dealt with by the message processor. In this situation, the message processor might cause the EMH to back away from the object.

Both Data and the EMH would have to have operating systems. Initially we would have said that the EMH could have existed as a subprogram of the main computer's operating system; however, the EMH can be downloaded into a mobile emitter which allows the EMH to exist beyond the confines of the ship's holographic projectors (e.g. outside of the Holodeck, or even outside the ship). Therefore, it is fair to say that the mobile emitter has its own operating system as it is an independent device. The EMH's program, therefore, exists as an autonomous program that can run on differing platforms. The EMH's program has also been transferred via an alien network from the Delta Quadrant to the *Prometheus* in the Alpha Quadrant in *VOY*: "Message in a Bottle," without any apparent effects to the EMH's operation. It is therefore more likely that Data, being a self contained computer, has an operating system that primarily handles the hardware aspect of the android and a program that handles the logical and computational side. The EMH, on the other hand, would simply be a transferable program designed to run on a number of differing operating systems. However, this program would have to be advanced to the point that it takes on most of the operating system functions. Rather than get bogged down with semantics, we will refer to the operating systems and programming of both Data and the EMH simply as a single program.

So what would this program do? As for all other computing devices, on start up the program would check internal and hardware settings. The program would examine the internal state of Data or the EMH and compare this state with the last known state, which would have been recorded by the program before it was shut down. This occurs in *STX: Insurrection*. Data experiences some kind of moral conflict between what he is being instructed to do and his programming. As a result Captain Picard and Lieutenant Commander Worf are forced to capture and shut Data down. Once back in Engineering on the *Enterprise*, Lieutenant Commander La Forge reactivates Data after having run his own set of diagnostics. On rebooting, Data notices right away that he is missing several memory engrams. Geordi La Forge holds up the computer chips for Data to see. On recognition of the chips Data says, "Oh, yes, there they are."

This is a perfect example of how an artificial life form's program should check its internal state and report any inconsistencies between the state before it was shut down and the new state. Of course problems with this methodology can still occur. During the shut down period it is possible that the internal state of the computer can be changed and false information inserted into the program in order to fool the program into thinking that it has not been tampered with.

This occurs to the EMH in *VOY*: "Latent Image," when Captain Janeway removes some memories from the EMH while he is deactivated. The memory loss is undetected by the EMH on reactivation. Janeway's measures worked for a while because the EMH could not detect something missing that he had no record of having in the first place. Although the EMH does not have hardware to check, his program would have saved files and data structures that contain his knowledge and working states. Having a complex program such as the EMH check the validity of all his past memories would be an arduous task and not something that would happen on the startup of a program. The EMH is oblivious to the deletion until he detects the scars of a past operation on Harry Kim with his own signature procedure but has no memory of performing it. Not only would his memories need to be erased but any physical evidence in the environment would also need to be covered up.

Once initial system checks have been performed and Data and the EMH have entered their main loop; their programming is in a perception mode, waiting for something to happen. This something may come in the form of one of two different event types: *external* or *internal*. An external event occurs when Data or the EMH must deal with a situation that directly affects them but originates outside of their physical being or program. This includes interaction with crew members, a command given by the captain, or the bulkheads falling down around them. Known in psychology as the stimulus-reflex behavior, for each external event that occurs Data and the EMH would be programmed with an appropriate response that would cause them to take action.

Of course, not all external events should cause a reflex action. If they did, the EMH would be forever ducking for cover. Besides the fact that it is impossible to program an artificial being to handle all situations that it may ever encounter throughout its life, it is also a waste of memory and programming subroutines. For example, programming the EMH to ignore Captain Janeway, although an unwise thing, would be pointless. To make the EMH or Data appear to ignore something is purely an exercise of omitting the subroutine to handle such events from their programming.

Internal events occur when the artificial being receives a message from its programming via subroutines that monitor its physical and mental states. One analogy in humans is hunger and, although Data and the EMH do not have a need for power recharging, other such beings would have subroutines that monitor their power levels and at certain times send messages to their message queues (a stimulus) that cause the being to take action to recharge (the reflex). In fact, although not entirely artificial, the Borg exhibit this type of behavior in their regeneration cycles.

When a program gets a message to ask it to shut down, it moves into the shutdown process. This process ensures that the current state of the program and hardware are stored for checking at startup. It would be wise programming practice to include a shutdown procedure when Data's off switch is pressed (as is demonstrated by Data himself to Dr. Crusher in *TNG*: "Datalore" and by Riker in *TNG*: "The Measure of a Man") and the EMH is deactivated.

FRAME OF MIND (*TNG#247*)

The operating system that we have just examined is a basic structure of processes that should exist at the lowest level of both Data and the EMH's programs. Extensions to their programming such as navigation, personality, and morality subroutines would be added on top. While the writing of such programs is beyond the scope of this book, we will examine the nature of the logic and data required to program such subroutines in the following chapters.

ENDNOTES

1. Of course this isn't an actual episode title, but a quote by the EMH that we just had to use.

2. A perfect example of how the EMH cannot expand beyond its original programming without the assistance of a programmer, because the EMH was never given the instructions on how it could modify the greeting itself. This would not have been a difficult thing to include; it's just that Dr. Zimmerman obviously never thought it was necessary.

CHAPTER 6

Representing and Storing Knowledge

CHAPTER OVERVIEW

Artificially intelligent beings aren't something that can be simply physically constructed, turned on, and expected to know everything. They need to be programmed with knowledge. Dr. Soong programmed Data with the memories of the inhabitants of the Omicron Theta Science Colony and Dr. Zimmerman programmed the EMH with medical knowledge taken from 3000 cultures and 47 surgeons. Encoding this type of information is no small feat. It is not simply a task of entering in blocks of text, but rather an exercise in structuring the knowledge in a way that it can be manipulated.

In this chapter we will examine the ways in which knowledge is structured in the field of AI and how these rules can be used to encode facts and processes into the brains of the EMH and Data.

11001001 (*TNG#116*)

Knowledge is more than just data or information. In AI fields, knowledge is considered to have two sides. On one side there is the stored information, and on the other, rules used to manipulate the information. This concept is illustrated well in *VOY*: "Message in a Bottle." In this episode, the EMH is sent as a holographic message via a complex alien network to the Alpha Quadrant. While he is away from the ship, Tom Paris is in charge of the sickbay. Not impressed with his role, he asks Harry Kim to help him create another EMH. Harry warns Tom it is a difficult task but eventually programs a hologram which looks exactly like the doctor. Harry then uploads the ship's entire medical library from *Gray's Anatomy of the Human Body*[1] to Leonard McCoy's *Comparative Alien Physiology*. Although Tom is quite optimistic about their attempts at creating a replacement EMH, Harry cautions him that being a doctor is about more than knowing all the facts. They will still have to program diagnostic analytical subroutines, tactile[2] protocols, and a personality profile. When the database upload is complete the replacement begins reciting text from *Gray's Anatomy* in a monotone. Their attempts at stopping the replacement's recitation results in an overload from all the uploaded data and the replacement hologram disintegrates.

This scenario illustrates two important concepts in AI. First, as we have already pointed out, information is not knowledge. Information is quite meaningless unless you know what to do with it. As Harry explains, the replacement EMH will need analytical subroutines in order to perform diagnosis. In other words, the replacement EMH needs to be programmed to use the uploaded information.

Second, the replacement EMH experiences an information overload from the vast quantity of uploaded data. Limited memory size seems to be an issue in the 24th century. There are many methods used for compressing and summarizing information in AI, and we will take a look at them while considering ways of representing knowledge.

SPOCK'S BRAIN (*TOS#061*)

Logic, as used by the Vulcans, is a method for reasoning about knowledge (or what we will call *facts*). In AI, logic is more; it is a way to represent facts as well-structured sentences. There are a number of logics used in AI, each with varying degrees of complexity and usefulness. We will take a quick look at a few.

Infinite Regress (*VOY#203*)

Propositional logic is the most simple form of logic, allowing for the storage of information and deductions on whether given information is true, false, or unknown. A fact is the simplest item in all logics. It can be likened to the database of data Harry uploaded into the EMH's memory. A simple set of facts for the EMH might include the following:

- a neural paralyser simulates death (*TOS*: "Amok Time")
- a neural neutralizer removes thoughts related to criminal acts (*TOS*: "Dagger of the Mind")
- an alpha-wave inducer eases the introduction of alpha waves into the brain (*DSN*: "The Passenger")
- the release of alpha-waves in the brain stimulates the patient (*DSN*: "The Passenger")

- nerve toxin immediately immobilises and kills the victim (*VOY*: "State of Flux")
- a hypospray delivers medication subcutaneously (*TOS*: "Miri")
- cordrazine is a potent stimulant (*TOS*: "The City on the Edge of Forever")
- kelotane is used to treat burns (*VOY*: "State of Flux")

As we noted before, all the factual information in the galaxy won't help the EMH diagnose his patients. We can start building a diagnostic analytical subroutine using what is known in logic as an *implication*. Implications have two sides. On the left is written the premise or list of facts, and on the right the conclusion. Therefore, the premises in the case of the EMH would be a list of symptoms, and the conclusion would be the diagnosis. Here is an example:

- (disease AND rapidly advancing AND adaptive AND highly resistant AND destroying genetic code AND destroying cellular structure) implies The Phage (*VOY*: "Phage")
- (disease AND effects blood AND degenerative AND caused by metreon isotopes AND may lie dormant for years AND attacks on the molecular level) implies metremia (*VOY*: "Jetrel")
- (paranoid delusions OR multi-infarct dementia) implies transporter psychosis (*TNG*: "Realm of Fear")
- (unconsciousness AND brain swelling) implies neural shock (*DSN*: "Equilibrium") OR encephalitis (*TNG*: "Future Imperfect" and *TNG*: "The Dauphin")

When facts are coupled with implications, it creates what is known as a knowledge base. A knowledge base is an extension of a database in that it contains not only data or facts, but also rules for using the data.

In the preceding examples, facts in the premise are coupled with logical connectives. In propositional logic there are five such connectives: *and*, *or*, *implies*, *equivalent*, and *not*. To understand how the connectives work, we need to examine Boolean algebra. Boolean algebra is something we might call the underlying language of the Vulcan race, for without it, logic could not exist.

Boolean algebra is based on values of *true* or *false*. Using the logical connectives we can add these values together to come up with true or false answers. A familiar tool in Boolean algebra is a truth table. This displays all the possible values for facts given a corresponding set of inputs as being true or false, and reveals what the resulting answer will be when the facts are combined using the connectives. Such a table is shown in Table 6.1.

TABLE 6.1   A Truth Table for Propositional Logic

A	B	not A	A and B	A or B	A implies B	A equals B
True	True	False	True	True	True	True
True	False	False	False	True	False	False
False	True	True	False	True	True	False
False	False	True	False	False	True	True

You can read Table 6.1 using the values of A and B in the first two columns. The remaining columns tell you what the answer will be when they are connected. For example, if A is true and B is true then A *and* B results in an answer of true (shown on the first line of Table 6.1. If you examine the table you will see that for facts connected with AND, both facts need to be true for the result to be true. For facts connected with an OR, a false is only obtained when both facts are false. For example, according to our EMH's diagnostic subroutine, *unconsciousness* and *brain swelling* are connected with an AND, meaning both symptoms have to be present or true for the implication of neural shock OR encephalitis to be true. In the case of transporter psychosis, the symptoms paranoid delusions and multi-infarct dementia are connected with an OR, and therefore only one need be present in order for the EMH to make a diagnosis.

Another logical connective is NOT. It simply changes the state of a fact from true to false or from false to true. For example, if the fact

  trianoline is a pain killer (*VOY*: "Caretaker, Part I")

were true then

  NOT(trianoline is a pain killer)

would be false.

As new facts are made known they are added to the knowledge base. When there are enough facts to match the entire premise of a rule, the rules can be calculated to be true or false. Until then, they remain unknown. Let's examine propositional logic in action. Imagine that on an away mission to Altair VI (*TOS:* "Amok Time") Worf and Dr. Crusher fail to report in at a prearranged time. Concerned, Captain Picard orders another away mission to find them. They are eventually found unconscious and beamed directly to sickbay. Because Dr. Crusher is out of action, the Emergency Medical Hologram aboard the *Enterprise-D* (*STIIX: First Contact*) is activated. The *Enterprise's* EMH jumps into action: *"Please state the nature of the medical emergency!"* We will reduce the EMH's knowledge base for illustrative purposes to the following:

R1:   unconscious implies neural shock OR Altairian encephalitis

R2:   Klingon implies NOT(Altairian encephalitis)

R3:   neural shock implies stimulant

R4:   stimulant implies cordrazine

We know that Klingons are immune to Altairian encephalitis (*TNG:* "Future Imperfect"), thus the inclusion of R2.

When Worf and Crusher arrive in sickbay, the EMH only has rules in his knowledge base, no facts. On examining Worf he can insert the fact:

F1:   unconscious.

When a fact is inserted it is assumed to be true. The EMH's diagnostic subroutine can now try and find rules with premises that match the fact. In this case R1 matches, so the conclusion of R1 becomes a fact, thus:

F2:   neural shock OR Altairian encephalitis.

At this point, the EMH has narrowed down his diagnosis to either neural shock or Altairian encephalitis. Because the conditions listed in F2 are connected with an OR, either one or both may be true for the entire fact to be true. To focus the diagnosis, the EMH needs more facts. He can also add into his knowledge base the fact that Worf is a Klingon, thus:

F3:   Klingon.

This in turn would fire R2 and insert the fact:

F4:   NOT(Altairian encephalitis).

If the diagnosis cannot be Altairian encephalitis, then it must be neural shock deducted from F2. This would activate R3 which in turn would activate R4 and the EMH would have diagnosed neural shock and also come up with a treatment. To further diagnose Crusher the EMH might apply a rule that states that whatever is wrong with Worf is probably the same thing that is wrong with Crusher, because they were found together in the same state.

Propositional logic works just fine in this simple example where the EMH is faced with symptoms that it knows about and only has one patient. But now imagine a sickbay full of crew members with differing conditions. Which one would the fact:

Klingon

be referring to? The EMH would need a further way of clarifying the preceding proposition with, for example:

$Klingon_{Worf}$

In this situation we have assumed there is only one Klingon aboard the *Enterprise-D*, but let's say there is an EMH stationed on Q'onoS (the Klingon homeworld). To now rule out Altairian encephalitis, the EMH would need a copy of R2 for each and every individual Klingon, thus:

$Klingon_{Worf} \Rightarrow$ NOT(Altairian encephalitis)

$Klingon_{K'Ehleyr} \Rightarrow$ NOT(Altairian encephalitis)

$Klingon_{Gowron} \Rightarrow$ NOT(Altairian encephalitis)

...

This would result in millions of rules just to say that every Klingon is immune from Altarian encephalitis.

Another problem with propositional logic is that it does not allow for change. In this example, the patient may have initially been unconscious; however, there is no way to indicate whether that is still the case. We would assume that once the EMH has administered the cordrazine that Worf and Crusher would need to regain consciousness, and the EMH has no way, using propositional logic, to remember when in the past the patient was unconscious or whether or not the cordrazine has been administered .

While these issues are not resolvable using propositional logic, they are with more advanced forms of logic.

Rules of Acquisition (*DSN#427*)

Whereas propositional logic only allows for the storage of propositions or facts, first-order logic allows for the storage of objects, properties about the objects, and relationships between the objects. For example, objects might include the following:

> James T. Kirk
>
> Dr. Leonard McCoy
>
> Spock
>
> Uhura

Relationships could be expressed thus:

> Superior(James T. Kirk, Uhura), said *James T. Kirk is the superior of Uhura.*
>
> Superior(Spock, Uhura), said *Spock is the superior of Uhura.*
>
> Friend(James T. Kirk, Spock), said *James T. Kirk is a friend of Spock.*

And properties might exist such as these:

> Half-Vulcan(Spock)
>
> Human(Uhura)
>
> Captain(James T. Kirk)

In addition to these, more information can be extrapolated by running functions on objects to query about their relationships and properties. For example:

> SuperiorOf(Dr Leonard McCoy)
>
> ChiefEngineerOf(*Enterprise*)
>
> etc.

First-order logic also has two powerful symbols called *quantifiers.* These allow the knowledge base to store generalizations and specializations about groups of objects in a single rule. In no particular order, the first is the existential qualification (∃). It allows us to make statements about any and every object in the knowledge base without naming it. To say, for example, that Yeoman Teresa Ross (*TOS*: "The Squire of Gothos") has a superior who is human, we would write

> ∃ × Superior(x,Ross) AND Human(x)

which pronounced states *There exists some object (which we will denote with x) which is the superior of Ross and is also human.* x is a place holder or variable and can take on any legitimate value. In propositional logic this one statement would have to be written out for every individual value of *x*, thus:

> Superior(James T. Kirk, Ross) AND Human(James T. Kirk)
>
> Superior(Uhura, Ross) AND Human(Uhura)
>
> Superior(Hikaru Sulu, Ross) AND Human(Hikaru Sulu)
>
> etc.

The second quantifier is the universal quantifier (∀). It allows for the expression of generalizations across the knowledge base. This is a good time to revisit our Klingon immunity rules from the previous section. Recall, in propositional logic the EMH would have to store a single rule for each individual Klingon stating that they could not have Altairian encephalitis. This might add several million rules to the knowledge base. Using the power of first-order logic's universal quantifier we can reduce this to just one rule. Essentially what we want the EMH to know is *all Klingons are immune to Altairian encephalitis.* And we can express that thus:

$\forall$x Klingon(x) implies Immune(Altairian encephalitis)

If the EMH has this in his knowledge base, then he can be assured that for all Klingons, no matter who they are, whatever their symptoms, they cannot possibly have Altairian encephalitis.

Shattered (*VOY#257*)

This has taken care of the first restriction we encountered in propositional logic. Now to address the second: temporal knowledge. One way of achieving this is to create a relationship called *Time* and use it thus:

Time(State(Worf, unconscious), Between(1100, 1200))

Time(Treatment(Worf, cordrazine), At(1155))

stating that Worf was in an unconscious state between 1100 and 1200 hours and was treated with cordrazine at 1155.

An extension of this that has become a logic in its own right is called Temporal logic. Rather than using the existing constructs of relationships, it has its own set of symbols for describing reactive and temporally dynamic environments. Temporal logic describes environmental states in an infinite sequence where each state has a successor.

Temporal logic attempts to define the relationships between time and events by specifically referring to times at which facts are true. Temporal logic extends propositional and first-order logic with a set of operators that refer to the past and the future. Some of the operators representing future truths are as follows:

Henceforth: This operator indicates a fact will be true from this time forward. For example, if someone passes their final exams at Starfleet Academy they will from that moment onward be an academy graduate.

Eventually: The eventually operator infers that a fact will be true sometime in the future. For example, Vulcan logic will eventually get the user into trouble.

Until: This operator suggests a fact will hold until another fact is true. For example, we would say a person will be alive until a nerve toxin is administered.

In addition to representing truths about the future, temporal logic also has a list of operators that express past truths. These include the following:

So-far: The so-far operator suggests a fact has been true up until this point in time; however, no conclusions can be made about its truth in the future. For example, Neelix's lung transplant (*VOY*: "Phage") has been successful so far.

Once: This operator allows for the writing of a fact that was once true but is no longer. For example, Kes had two lungs before donating one to Neelix; thus we could say, Kes once had two lungs.

The previously defined operators relate to the concept of linear time in which time is considered to be a single line beginning at some time index 0 and continuing infinitely into the future. This form of temporal logic is called *Linear Temporal Logic*. A second type of temporal logic called *Branching Temporal Logic* considers the possibility of multiple futures and can conceptually be represented as a tree beginning at a single root point in time and branching out in all directions. Branching temporal logic makes use of the linear temporal logic operators as well as two extras. These are an operator for *all futures* and one for *some futures*. Consider this sentence:

All Starfleet Academy students who study hard will eventually graduate.

In Branching Temporal Logics this could be rewritten as:

All Starfleet Academy students who study hard **will** eventually graduate.

or

> All Starfleet Academy students who study hard **may** eventually graduate.

Now you might be thinking that Branching Temporal Logic would be absolutely ideal for the knowledge base of an AI in *Star Trek* because of all the time travel and multiple dimensions, but it can also be quite useful for an EMH aware of just one timeline. It is a way of summarising the uncertainty in the results obtained in medical treatments. In *VOY*: "Threshold," Janeway and Paris undergo a speedy evolutionary process that turns them into, for want of a better description, giant slimy slugs. The EMH destroys the mutated DNA with an antiproton radiation treatment (ART). Because this treatment worked the EMH could conclude:

> Individuals experiencing mutated DNA who are treated with ART will eventually have no mutated DNA no matter what occurs after the treatment.

If, however, there was some subsequent requirement (for instance, the patient has to remain lying down after the treatment) that the EMH could not predict the patient adhering to, he might modify the previous logic to only some futures. There might also be a number of other things that could happen after the treatment but before the mutated DNA is fully removed that could prevent the success of the treatment that are currently unknown to the EMH and unpredictable. To err on the side of caution, it is probably best never to assume anything will hold for *all* futures.

RETROSPECT (*VOY#185*)

In this chapter we have examined a number of ways in which to structure logic and make reasonable deductions. These structures are paramount in the field of AI for empowering artificial beings with knowledge about facts and processes. However, as we will examine in Part III, it might just be the nature of the logic examined in this chapter that defines the limitations of

AI. For example, in *TOS*: "I, Mudd," the *Enterprise* and its crew escape from a planet of clingy androids by causing the head android to malfunction by confusing it with a logical paradox.

This aside, the techniques discussed herein are commonly used today in the fields of AI and A-Life with great success. There is no doubt that they would be very useful in creating artificial intelligences for Data, the EMH and the plethora of other AI identities in *Star Trek*.

ENDNOTES

1. A complete reference of human anatomy written by Henry Gray in 1918.
2. A sense of touch.

Thinking and Reasoning

CHAPTER OVERVIEW

Programming knowledge into an artificial being is an arduous job. Imagine trying to write out everything that you know. Not a task we would contemplate! Even using the logic languages given in the previous chapter, there would still be a lot of facts and rules to write. An extension of this work is to give the AI rules and knowledge that help it to learn and program it with methods that it can use to create and enter new knowledge into its database.

In the previous chapter we saw how data and information can be presented in a specialized format called logic. Logic is the basis on which computers are built and programmed. It will be no different for the artificial intelligences of the 24th century. In this chapter we will go one step up from logic and look at how it is used in the programming of artificial intelligences.

ELEMENTARY, DEAR DATA (*TNG#129*)

It is by Data's very nature that he uses deductions to solve problems and make decisions. Geordi alludes to it being Data's greatest strength in *TNG*: "Elementary Dear Data," when Data takes on the role of one of earth history greatest literary heroes, Sherlock Holmes. Holmes himself was also known for his outward display of the deductive reasoning process. Unfortunately, as Dr. Kathryn Pulaski points out in the same episode, Data lacks one insight that Holmes possesses: an understanding of the human soul. Although from what we learn about Data on his journey to become human, Pulaski's comments about his abilities are somewhat harsh. As we learn from the moment she meets him in *TNG*: "The Child," she is brazenly forward with her attitude of Data being just a *machine,* and at one point describes him as *the cold hand of technology.*

While Data's reasoning is a continuous operation of his positronic brain, we sometimes witness striking evidence of the processes. In *TNG*: "Lonely Among Us," the *Enterprise* is under a systems attack by some unknown force. Data makes the simple deduction that the *Enterprise* couldn't simply be malfunctioning because it is fragile, otherwise Starfleet would never have let it leave the dock. He therefore concludes that there must be a saboteur on board. Before we continue with our examination of Data's deductions, let's take a quick look at the formal side of this reasoning technique.

Tuvix (*VOY#140*)

A deductive argument is one that provides one or two assertions or facts that lead to a conclusion. This is the same technique used in the previous chapter on logic that allowed us to conclude if one fact was true and it implied another fact, then that second fact must also be true. Before other types of logic were codified, logic consisted only of deductive reasoning, which concerns what follows universally from given truths. The traditional logic used for deductions is called Aristotelian logic, also known as *syllogistics*, created by Aristotle. Such a logic statement contains an *antecedent* and a *consequent*. The antecedent is stated first and usually describes an object, person, or other entity. The consequent follows and describes some property of the antecedent. For example, a simple syllogism would be

All Vulcans are logical,

with *All Vulcans* being the antecedent and *are logical* being the consequent.

Okay, so this statement is seriously generalized. When Vulcans let their suppressed emotions get the better of them they do often act rather illogically (*STI: Star Trek The Motion Picture* and *VOY*: "Blood Fever"). This usually occurs during the *pon farr*; a mating drive experienced every seven years in a male Vulcan's life. There is also a group of Vulcans that have rejected the *kohlinar discipline* (emotion-purging training) called *V'tosh ka'tur* (*ENT*: "Fusion"), or *Vulcans without Logic,* who pilgrimage across the galaxy to find a balance between emotion and logic. However, for illustrative purposes we will stick with *All Vulcans are logical.*

Aristotle came up with four statements that could be used in his logic, thus:

- every x is a y   (the universal affirmative)
- no x is a y   (the universal negative)
- some x is a y   (particular affirmative)
- not every x is a y   (particular negative)

Given these statements, a classical syllogistic might be:

> If every x is a y
> and every y is a z,
> then every x is a z[1].

An example of this type of syllogistic might be:

> If every EMH is a hologram
> and every hologram is a projection of light,
> then every EMH is a projection of light.

No matter which type of logic you are dealing with, the process of deductive reasoning can always be applied. Such a technique of coming to a conclusion given a premise or two is said to be deductively valid if and only if there is no possible situation in which all the premises are true and the conclusion false.

For example, if the EMH has the two premises

1. *All Vulcans have green blood.*
2. *Tuvok is a Vulcan.*

and concluded:

> *Tuvok has blue blood,*

it would be invalid deductive reasoning.

In simple two premise syllogisms, like the preceding, the second (or minor) premise can relate in four different ways to the first (or major) premise, but only two of the ways produces sound deductive reasoning. The first sound way is called *affirming the antecedent*. This means that the minor premise's antecedent must relate to an instance of the antecedent in the major premise. For example, if

> *All Vulcans are logical.*
> *Tuvok is a Vulcan.*

then

> *Tuvok is logical.*

The second way to ensure a sound deductive argument is to *deny the consequent*. This means the minor premise must indicate that its antecedent does not equate to the consequent of the major premise. For example, if:

> *All Vulcans are logical.*
> *B'lanna Torres is not logical.*

then

> *B'lanna Torres is not Vulcan.*

The third way a minor premise can relate to a major premise is called *affirming the consequent*. This means making a conclusion based on the consequent of the minor and major premises being the same. This type of reasoning makes for a deductive fallacy. For example, if:

> *All Vulcans are logical.*
> *Data is logical.*

then

> *Data is a Vulcan.*

This is simply not true. It is the equivalent of making some huge and incorrect generalisation and modifying the first premise to say something like *everything that is logical is a Vulcan*, which, we know, is not true.

Last but not least, the fourth way to relate minor and major premises, called *denying the antecedent*, also results in a deductive fallacy. This occurs when the minor premise asserts that its antecedent is not an instance of the major premise's antecedent. For example, if:

All Vulcans are logical.
Data is not a Vulcan.

then

Data is not logical.

Besides the preceding two premise relationships there are two other ways that premises can lead to unsound deductions. The first is called *ambiguity*. This is when a word or phrase is present in both premises but has a different meaning. For example, if:

Starships have special shielding to protect them from hot bodies in space.
Seven of Nine has a hot body.

then

A starship's shielding should protect it from Seven of Nine.

A great example of this type of logic is demonstrated in *VOY*: "Riddles." Neelix poses a question to Tuvok similar to, "If an ensign is stranded on a desolate inhospitable planet with nothing but a calendar, how is it that a year later a rescue team finds him alive and well fed?" When Neelix reveals that the answer to the riddle is that the ensign survived by eating the dates on the calendar, Tuvok exclaimed that Neelix's logic was flawed and merely wordplay. And indeed it is, as well as a perfect example of an ambiguous deduction.

The final cause of a deductive fallacy is *division*. This occurs when the major premise is a generalisation and does not necessarily apply to individual cases. For example, if:

Humanoids are common in every area of the delta quadrant.
Cardassians are humanoids.

then

> *Cardassians are common in every area of the delta quadrant.*

Now it is possible that deductive fallacies might equate to true in some circumstances. For example, if:

> *Holograms are a projection of light.*
> *The EMH is a hologram.*

then

> *The EMH is a projection of light.*

However, we are sure that they cannot be assumed correct for all premises and conclusions and therefore are not trusted.

The Voyager Conspiracy (*VOY#229*)

Let's have a look at some deductive reasoning gone wrong. An excellent example can be found in *VOY*: "The Voyager Conspiracy." In this episode, Seven of Nine attempts to assimilate *Voyager's* reports and sensor data in order to process it in a manner more efficient than simply reading it. We can consider Seven of Nine as an artificial intelligence because, although she is human, simply uploading data from a computer is not something a normal human can do. It is therefore her artificial component, the Borg implant, that is digesting the information.

On her first attempt, after assimilating six months of the ship's status reports, she comes to the conclusion that there are a mating pair of photonic fleas in the sensor grid and possibly their offspring are disrupting its power flow. When Captain Janeway asks how she came to the conclusion, Seven reasons thus:

- *Eight weeks ago an away team encountered a Kartellan freighter from which Neelix acquired some amber spice.*
- *On the same day Ensign Kim was preparing a replicator in the mess hall.*

■ *Amber spice is a nesting place for photonic fleas.*
■ *Photonic fleas eat plasma particles.*
■ *The conduit of the sensor grid near the replicator contains an unlimited supply of plasma particles.*
■ *The sensor grid was exposed when the replicator was being repaired.*
■ *Periodically the sensor emitters momentarily lose resolution.*

Tuvok insists that, while Seven's analysis is logical, it is also highly speculative. We might take this to mean that there are some deductive fallacies lurking in Seven's logic. For example, most of Seven's logic contains facts such as the encounter with the Kartellan freighter; however, there is one syllogism that could cause a problem. Here it is:

Neelix has amber spice.
Amber spice is a nesting place for photonic fleas.

Then

Neelix has photonic fleas.

This syllogism is an example of a deductive division, because the second premise does not mean that *all* amber spice contains photonic fleas. Therefore, though Seven's suspicions turned out to be true in this case, they might not always.

Coming up with a value of probability to apply to premises can be determined using *inductive reasoning*. This type of reasoning studies the derivation of reliable generalizations from a series of observations. For example, Seven would have been better off gathering some statistical data about the occurrences of photonic fleas in amber spice. If, for example, photonic fleas exist in 20 percent of amber spice containers, then she could only be 20 percent certain that Neelix was in possession of some. As inductive reasoning dives into the realm of statistical analysis we will end our discussion of it here.

Examining inductive reasoning nicely introduces us to an area of logical reasoning not dealt with in propositional or first-order logic: the concept of uncertainty. In our previous example of an EMH's diagnostic analytical subroutine, we considered simple black and white diagnosis. Unfortunately, as anyone who knows medicine will tell you, real medical diagnoses aren't always this easy. There is often a lot of uncertainty in the equation, and you often cannot say whether something is 100 percent true or false. We therefore need some way of representing knowledge in degrees of belief so we can say things like *I am 80 percent sure this is the case*. First-order logic is incapable of this type of knowledge representation; however, the next type of logic we are going to look at thrives on it.

PATTERNS OF FORCE (*TOS#052*)

Uncertainty is something that humans have to deal with every day. When making decisions, we are often given incomplete, inconsistent, or imperfect information with which to reason. Somehow we manage to deal with such situations. Computers, however, tend to deal in true and false answers (as illustrated in the previous sections), and therefore have difficulty with information that is deficient. One logic process that deals with uncertainty is *Bayesian inferencing*. It attempts to handle reasoning under uncertain conditions and is modelled on the way that we reason in these situations implementing probability theory.

Probability deals with the chances of some event occurring or some fact being true. Probability is expressed mathematically as a real number between 0 and 1, where an occurrence with probability of 0 means that it will never happen, and a probability of 1 means that it will definitely happen. A probability of 1 can also be construed as an absolute *success*, whereas a probability of 0 can be taken to mean an absolute *failure*. The probability of success can be expressed as

$$p(success) = \frac{number\_of\_past\_sucesses}{number\_of\_attempts}$$

and the probability of failure as

$$p(failure) = \frac{number\_of\_past\_sucesses}{number\_of\_attempts}.$$

For example, Lieutenant Tuvok may have hit Kazon ships with *Voyager's* phasers 3050 times out of 3450 attempts. His probability for successfully striking the Kazon is therefore 3050/3450 = 0.88, or, to put it another way, he has an accuracy of 88 percent. The probability that he will not hit a Kazon ship can be calculated from the fact that the probability of success plus the probability of failure always equals 1, thus:

$$p(success) + p(failure) = 1.$$

Therefore, Tuvok's failure rate is 0.12, or 12 percent.

Probably the most outspoken AI to use probability would have to be the Cardassian weapon of mass destruction, *Dreadnought* (*VOY*: "Dreadnought"). When the crew of *Voyager* detected this self-propelled weapon in the Delta quadrant, B'lanna Torres and Chakotay admitted to having reprogrammed the weapon with a new identity in the Alpha quadrant to attack the Cardassians. Unfortunately, it had now found its way into the Delta quadrant and was determined to destroy its target, Rakosa, a massively populated planet that it had mistaken for Ashalon 5, a Cardassian fuel depot.

Torres transports over to *Dreadnought* in order to deactivate it. The weapon scans and identifies her before allowing her access to its systems. Torres asks *Dreadnought* to confirm its target. It informs her that it thinks it is heading for Ashalon 5 and believes it is the correct target based on size, radio thermic signature, and atmospheric composition. Torres tries to tell the weapon that it is no where near Ashalon 5, and it responds by telling her that, based on its available data, she is mistaken. After repairing the weapon's sensors, Torres asks it to reinitialize its navigational systems. The weapon is then asked to verify its current position which it determines to be in the Delta quadrant. It then reasons with Torres that its target is not Ashalon 5 and it shuts down its systems. Torres returns to *Voyager*. Shortly after, the weapon resumes its mission to destroy what it thinks is Ashalon 5. Torres is perplexed and queries the weapon's computer on its motivation. Its response is that Torres has entered false information into its sensor array.

This episode presents a particularly interesting concept in logic, and at this point we will briefly reinvestigate first-order logic. We could assume that *Dreadnought* possesses knowledge such as[2]:

```
F1:  size(target, 11000km)
F2:  radiothermic(target, 50 degrees)
F3:  atmosphere(target, 50% nitrogen 50% oxygen)
F4:  location(target, alpha quadrant)
F5:  location(dreadnought, alpha quadrant)

R1:    size(target, 11000km) AND
       radiothermic(target, 50 degrees) AND
       atmosphere(target, 50% nitrogen 50% oxygen) AND
       location(target, alpha quadrant)
       implies name(target, ashalon 5)
R2:    name(target, ashalon 5) AND
       location (dreadnought, alpha quadrant)implies
       destroy(target)
```

Having verified the first four facts, R1 would be fired, thus inserting the new fact

```
F6:  name(target, ashalon 5).
```

This, in turn, would fire R2, and *Dreadnought* would assume its objective was to destroy the target. Now Torres comes along and gives *Dreadnought* the new fact

```
F6:  location(dreadnought, delta quadrant).
```

As *Dreadnought* is capable of navigation, we might assume it has a rule that explains to it that it cannot be in two places, thus:

```
R3:    ∀ dreadnought,x,y  implies
       NOT( location(dreadnought,x) AND at(dreadnought,y) )
```

or, in other words, for all places located at x and y, *Dreadnought* cannot be in both.

Therefore, when F6 is added it will negate F5; thus R2 becomes false, and the weapon should remove the fact destroy(target) as its objective. And this is what Torres assumed it had done. Unfortunately, the weapon was programmed to be a little smarter than this, and when it detected the conflict in its knowledge base caused by R3, it began another reasoning process.

We later learn that when Torres reprogrammed the weapon, she added a tactical subroutine to watch for 39 threats to its programming. *Dreadnought* assessed the entry of false information into its sensor array as an indicator that there was a threat. Knowing this, *Dreadnought* assessed that the most probable cause of the threat was that Torres had been captured and coerced by Cardassian forces to disable it. How did it determine which of the 39 threats was occurring?

To illustrate how Bayesian inference can be used to represent and solve this problem, we will reduce the number of threats down to a more manageable three:

- Torres has been captured and coerced by Cardassians.
- Torres has joined forces with the Cardassians.
- The war with the Cardassians is over.

Of course there could be other types of threats such as computer malfunction, Borg assimilation, etc.; however, these might not involve Torres and would add an extra level of difficulty to our example, by making it first necessary to detect who was doing the sabotage.

The probability of an event, *E*, might also be expressed as the ratio of desired outcomes to all outcomes as expressed as

$$p(E) = \frac{number\_of\_desired\_outcomes}{number\_of\_possible\_outcomes}.$$

For example, a die has six numbers on it. The probability of rolling a 5 is 1/6, or 0.167, where the number of desired outcomes is 1 (because there is only one 5 on a die) and the number of possible outcomes is 6 (as the die has 6 sides). Outcomes that can occur with the throwing of a die (1, 2, 3, 4, 5, or 6) are independent and mutually exclusive, because we cannot obtain, for example, a 6 and a 3 in the same roll. However, it is often the case that events are not independent, and the outcome of one event can influence the outcome of another event. For instance, the probability that Torres entered false information into *Dreadnought* is influenced by the probability that she was coerced by the Cardassians, which is influenced by the probability that she was captured by them. In this case, we consider *conditional probability*, which examines the probability of event *A* occurring if event *B* occurs or vice versa. This is written as

$$p(A|B)$$

and pronounced the *probability of A occurring if B has already occurred.*
   This type of reasoning leads to what is called the *Bayesian Rule*, or

   if   A is true

   then   B is true with probability p.

   This implies that if event *A* occurs, then the probability of *B* occurring is *p*. This would lead *Dreadnought* to consider questions such as, *If false information has been entered into my sensors, then what is the probability that Torres has been coerced by Cardassians?* With Bayesian inferencing the rule can be reversed to, *If Torres has been coerced by Cardassians, what is the probability that she will enter false information into my sensors?* This allows for human-like reasoning that can make conclusions about the *effects from causes* or the *causes from effects.*
   Thus far we have examined one event dependent on one other; however, what if an event was dependent on multiple mutually exclusive events? For example, would the probability of *Dreadnought's* sensor's being compromised be higher if Torres was captured by the Cardassians *and* she decided to join forces with them? Such a probability would be written as

$$p(A|[B,C])$$

or *the probability of A occurring if both B and C have already occurred.*
   Table 7.1 examines some potential probabilities associated with the threats to *Dreadnought's* mission and how it might come to some conclusion about what caused the entry of false information. For this table we are assuming the probability of B'lanna being captured is 45%, B'lanna joining forces with the Cardassians is 1% and the war being over 20%. Hence, the

probability of B'lanna not being captured is 55%, B'lanna not joining with the Cardassians is 99% and the war not being over 80%.

TABLE 7.1   The probabilities of events leading to Dreadnought's sensor compromise

1	2	3	4	5[a]
Captured & Coerced	Joined Cardassians	War is Over	Sensors Compromised Because 1, 2 and/or 3 Has Occurred	Probability of Sensor Compromise
45%[b]	**1%**	**20%**	0.01%	0.00%
45%	**1%**	80%	20%	0.07%
45%	99%	**20%**	20%	1.80%
45%	99%	80%	30%	11.0%
55%	**1%**	**20%**	0.5%	0.00%
55%	**1%**	80%	90%	0.30%
55%	99%	**20%**	90%	10.0%
55%	99%	80%	0.01%	0.00%

[a] Column 5 = Column 1 x Column 2 x Column 3 x Column 4

[b] Bolded values indicate the probability of an event being true, unbolded is the probability of an event being false.

Here, we are saying that the probabilities of Torres being captured and coerced (Column 1) is 45%, of Torres joining forces with the Cardassians (Column 2) is 1%, and of the war being over is 20%. These values are represented in Table 7.1 in the respective columns in bolded text. Because the probability of something occurring is being considered, we also need to consider the probability of that something won't occur. For example, the probability that Torres will not be captured is 55%, or 1 minus the probability that she will be captured. These are the values not bolded in Table 7.1. Note that the values for the columns have not been calculated, but are simply values we made up for this example. In a real life example, these values would be obtained from the opinions of experts or from some scientific experimentation. In the first line of Table 7.1, therefore, we are saying we think that column 1, independent of anything else, is 45%. The probabilities of column 2 and column 3 are considered in the same way. The value of column 4 is determined by considering the question, *What would the probability of sensor compromise occurring be if all of the following have occurred: Torres has been captured AND joined Cardassian forces AND the war is over.* On the second line of the table, we are saying that the war being over has not occurred (notice it is not bolded) and hence the fourth column is considering the question, *What would the probability of sensor compromise occurring be if B'lanna has been captured AND joined Cardassian forces?*

Now, given all these expert evaluations of Torre's convictions and ability to avoid capture, etc., we can calculate some values for the probability of the event (in this case, entry of false information into *Dreadnought*) occurring. In this example, the most likely explanation for the false information is Torres' capture and coercion alone (shown underlined in Table 7.1) followed closely by the war being over.

We are certain the majority of AIs in *Star Trek* calculate and use probabilities to make many decision. For example, the EMH would have to use probabilities when treating illnesses when the cause was unknown, because the treatment might depend on the cause. For instance, consider a patient who is taken to sickbay with the symptoms of a flu. How could the EMH determine what type of flu it is if all known types exhibit the same symptoms in the early stages? Could it be Artethian flu (*VOY:* "Eye of the Needle"), Levodian flu (*VOY:* "Tattoo"), Thelusian flu (*TNG:* "Unnatural Selection"), Urodelan flu *(TNG:* "Genesis") or Karmaraazite flu (*ENT:* "Sleeping Dogs")? The EMH would have to take into consideration who the patient is, who else on the crew has had similar symptoms, where the patient has been, etc., and then he could not be 100% certain. What the EMH decides could make all the difference to the treatment, and if he treated the flu with the wrong therapy, it could have detrimental effects.

TRIALS AND TRIBBLE-ATIONS (*DSN#503*)

Computer programmers are used to working with discrete answers of true and false. But how often do you answer a question with a *yes* or *no*? If someone asked you, *How often do you watch Star Trek?*, you might answer, *Always, Most of the time, Sometimes,* or *Hardly ever*. In this case, not only are you giving a yes answer, but you are also specifying a degree of truth. As we have seen, logic uses discrete distinctions for properties. For example, the statement *It is always hot on Vulcan* could not be expressed in first-order logic because the term *hot* is too subjective and ambiguous, and it could refer to a range of actual temperature values. However, if we said that something is hot if it is over 50°C (122 °F), then we could propose:

> *The temperature on Vulcan is hot.*
>
> *It's temperature is always 50 °C or above.*

Because we are working with sharp distinctions, does this mean that any planet with a temperature of 50°C or less is cold? Of course, you could add another category of temperature such as warm to make a more sensible scale; however, the cut-off values would still create harsh divisions. *Fuzzy logic* can help avoid such logicalities.

Fuzzy logic provides a way to infer a conclusion based upon vague, ambiguous, inaccurate, and incomplete information. Humans work with these restrictions in making decisions, and from one human to another there is an unspoken agreement as to the interpretation of a vague statement. As vague terminology is often used by many people to express knowledge, it seems inevitable that a language should exist that allows a computer to understand knowledge fed to it in this format. Fuzzy logic is based on the concept that properties can be described on a sliding scale. For example, when spoken about, properties such as temperature, height, and speed are often described with terms such as *too hot, very tall,* or *really slow* respectively.

Fuzzy logic works by applying the theory of sets to describe the range of values that exists in vague terminologies. Classical set theory from mathematics (as used in the section on first-order logic) provides a way of specifying whether some entity is a member of a set or not. For example, given the temperatures $a = 55$ (131°F), and $b = 34$ (93.2°F), and the set called *Hot* which includes all numerical values equal to and greater than 50, we could say that a is a member of the set *Hot* with the notation

$a \in Hot$

and say that b is not a member of the set *Hot* with

$b \notin Hot.$

Classical set theory forces lines to be drawn between categories, which produces distinct true and false answers. For example, *Member(b, Hot)* must equate to false in classical theory. What fuzzy logic does is blur the borderlines between sets (make them fuzzy!). This is achieved with fuzzy set theory. While classical set theory operates with only two values, true (1) and false (0), fuzzy set theory works with a range of real values between 0 and 1. Instead of an entity being a member or not being a member of a set, fuzzy set theory allows for a degree of membership (DOM). This can best be explained with the following example.

In *TNG*: "The Quality of Life," Dr. Farallon asks Data to give her an initial assessment of the exocomps. Data responds by classifying their abilities as *excellent*. Now, instead of describing them like this, Data could have gone to great lengths to describe their power consumption, learning, speed of work, etc., but instead he chose to say they were excellent. Dr. Farallon seemed most satisfied with his classification of the exocomps. We can assume from this that Dr. Farallon and Data shared a common understanding of the somewhat vague term of *excellent*. In this case, it satisfactorily summarized Data's assessment. It is one thing for a human to understand such fuzzy terminology, but how can Data process it? Let's assume Data has two other terms that he could have selected from to classify the exocomp performance, unsatisfactory and fair. For illustration purposes, we will also reduce the set of characteristics by which Data is assessing the exocomps to include only power consumption. Therefore, we would basically be asking Data to rate the exocomp's power consumption as unsatisfactory, fair, or excellent. Fuzzy classification begins with a measured value. In the previous example of *Hot*, the temperature was measured; in this case we need an exact value for power consumption. Let's say Data measures the exocomp's power consumption at 10 kilowatts per hour. In order for Data to determine the classification for this value, he must already possess knowledge of the fuzzy sets for unsatisfactory, fair, and excellent. When drawn, fuzzy sets look mostly triangular. Examples of some fuzzy sets for Data are shown in Figure 7.1.

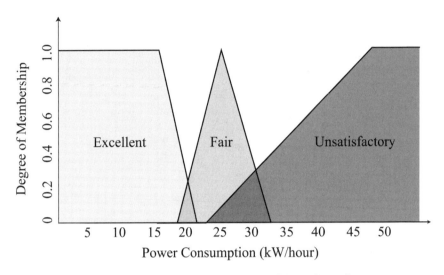

FIGURE 7.1   Example fuzzy sets for unsatisfactory, fair, and excellent.

Notice in Figure 7.1 the sets are defined by the axes *Power Consumption* and *Degree of Membership*. The first is our measurable value, and the second is what distinguishes fuzzy sets from normal ones. In fuzzy set theory, values don't just belong to a set, they have a degree of membership. In Figure 7.1, we can see from the graph for the *Excellent* set that a power consumption of 10kW has a degree of membership of 1.0. On the other hand, a value of 20kW has a membership of 0.25 in the *Excellent* set and 0.25 in the *Fair* set. Each set is defined by a line describing the top boundary of the set's shape. This line is defined as a set of points given as a pair of values for the degree of membership followed by the measured value, in this case, the power consumption written as degree of membership/power consumption. The sets in Figure 7.1 can therefore be written as

> Excellent = { 0/0, 1/16, 0/22 }
>
> Fair = { 0/19, 1/25, 0/33 }
>
> Unsatisfactory = { 0/23, 1/43 }.

The next step in fuzzy logic is to combine these sets within logical rules to be used in reasoning. Let's say that Data has the following rules for determining the overall performance of the exocomps:

If work speed is fast

and power consumption is fair,

then performance is satisfactory.

If work speed is slow

and power consumption is unsatisfactory,

then performance is unsatisfactory.

Figure 7.2 illustrates each of the fuzzy sets for power consumption, work speed, and performance, where each measured value is given as a percentage.

Using these sets and some initial measurements of work speed and power consumption, Data could come up with a fuzzy classification for performance. There are a couple of methods that could be used, but we will illustrate the simplest technique, called Mamdani-style. This technique is executed in four steps:

1. **Fuzzification.** This involves taking a measured value and turning it into a fuzzy classification. Let's proceed by assuming that Data has measured the exocomp's work speed at 45% and their power consumption at 65%. These values are projected into the fuzzy sets as shown in Figure 7.2. They result in work speeds of 0.4 slow, 0.2 fast, and power consumptions 0.2 fair, 0.2 unsatisfactory, respectively.
2. **Evaluation.** Next, these degrees of membership for each value are used to assess the degree of membership for the performance classification. To determine this, we need to know a little more about fuzzy logic. Note that both the rules we have been given combine the premises with the word *and*. The alternative is to combine them with another logical connector such as *or* (as examined in the section on propositional logic). In short, when an

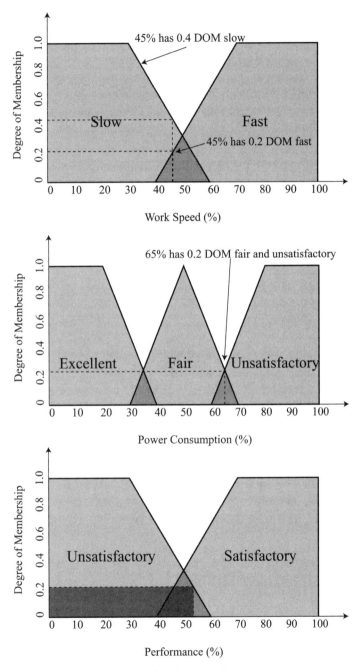

FIGURE 7.2 Fuzzy sets and their use in fuzzy reasoning.

and is used, the minimum degree of membership is allocated to the conclusion, and when an *or* is used, the maximum degree of membership is allocated. Therefore, in this case we have thus far determined:

- *Work speed is (0.2) fast **and** power consumption is (0.2) fair, then performance is (0.2) satisfactory.*
- *Work speed is (0.4) slow **and** power consumption is (0.2) unsatisfactory, then performance is (0.2) unsatisfactory.*

Because they are connected with an *and*, the degree of membership of the performances will be the minimum value from each rule. In this case they are the same.

3. **Aggregation.**   The next step takes the degree of freedom determined for the performance and uses it to clip the size of the performance fuzzy set. This is shown in Figure 7.2 as the darkened area in the bottom left of the graph. This is the region of the whole performance set where both unsatisfactory and satisfactory have 0.2 degree of membership.

4. **Defuzzification.**   The final step is to take the clipped part of the performance graph and determine a value. The simplest method for doing this is called the centroid technique. This basically finds the vertical line that would cut the clipped area exactly in half (volume wise). In this case, we have ended up with a rectangle which makes the calculation quite easy. The width of the clipped area is 52; we can therefore say that the value of performance for a work speed of 45% and a power usage of 65% is 26% or, if we refuzzify according to Figure 7.2, the performance of the exocomp is unsatisfactory.

ALL GOOD THINGS... *(TNG#277, 288)*

In this chapter we have examined several methods which enable artificial intelligences to reason about the knowledge they possess. From deductive reasoning based on facts to dealing with uncertainty and vagueness with Bayesian inferencing and fuzzy logic, there are many techniques to select from with which to program such a being with the ability to think and reason.

In the next chapter, the final for this Part, we will examine some methods at the forefront of AI that are allowing artificial beings to learn, adapt, and evolve.

ENDNOTES

1. A famous syllogistic called The Barbara Syllogistic.
2. We have taken a little artistic license of our own with the values selected here.

CHAPTER 8

Beyond Their Original Programming

CHAPTER OVERVIEW

Not an episode of *Voyager* goes by when we don't hear the EMH or a crew member comment on how he has exceeded his original programming. "Quite a task," you might think, given the state of today's computers, but not entirely impossible. The way this capacity would be bestowed upon an artificial being would be to give it the ability to learn. In considering this, we need to address two issues. First, are we simply allowing the AI to collect more knowledge by increasing the size of its memory, or second, are we allowing it to reprogram itself?

The program of an AI, like any other computer program, is the software loaded into the machine that runs continuously while the machine is turned on or the AI is activated[1]. Programs are written by programmers in the form of programming code. When finished, the code is converted into a format the computer can understand (machine code) and then run. For a program to rewrite itself, it would have to have a complete understanding of its program. We might liken this to a person knowing exactly how he is constructed from the cellular level. This would be easier for a program to achieve because it would only have to study the portion of computer memory that it was loaded into to get a holistic image of itself.

In order for the program to reprogram itself, it would have to be programmed with the necessary routines to tell it *how* to reprogram itself. If the original programmer did not have the insight to predict all the possible future programming needs of the program, how will the program know how to reprogram itself for any particular new situation? For example, we can't truly believe that Dr. Lewis Zimmerman programmed the EMH with the ability to program itself to sing opera, can we? The EMH may be encoded with elementary sequences that allow it to program devices such as medical tricorders, but could it use these basics to, say, reprogram itself to re-create the works of Da Vinci?

If we examine the way in which humans better themselves, it is not by chopping off an arm then creating a better one and sewing it on. It doesn't work like that. We cannot re-create our physical selves as better models (no matter what plastic surgeons may tell us). We have to work with what we have been given, and that is a set of instructions for manipulating our bodies and minds. Today some programs are written with a similar set of instructions that don't allow them to rewrite their base code (likened to our bodies), but do allow them to manipulate the order in which instructions are executed to change their behavior. For example, many computer game programs today come with what is called a *game engine*. Instead of allowing novices to hack around with the base code, computer game developers create scripting languages. These are simplistic[2] (though sometimes complex) instructions for creating new games from the original and manipulating the way the original program works. It does not, however, allow the original game to be rewritten. Some games even write their own scripts and thus allow them to seemingly change themselves, although it isn't truly the case.

For any AI to exceed beyond its original programming, to be able to rewrite its program to deal with new situations or improve itself, it needs the ability to adapt. In other words, it originally needs to be programmed with the ability to learn. This is achieved using a method similar to that explained earlier, where the program doesn't actually rewrite its base code, but creates new subroutines that it can run.

Two methods in AI that allow programs to search for problem solutions and create their own set of instructions and subroutines are genetic algorithms and genetic programming. These reside in the AI domain of *evolutionary computing*.

EVOLUTION (*TNG#150*)

Evolutionary computing is an AI technique used in programming learning and the discovery of optimal solutions for problem solving. It examines intelligence through environmental adaptation and survival and attempts to simulate the process of natural evolution by implementing concepts such as selection, reproduction, and mutation. In short, it endeavors to computationally replicate the genetic process involved in biological evolution.

Genetics, or the study of heredity, concentrates on the transmission of traits from parents to offspring. It not only examines how physical characteristics such as hair and eye color are passed to the next generation, but it also observes the transmission of behavioral traits such as temperament and intelligence [Lefton94]. All cells in all living beings, with the exception of some viruses, store these traits in *chromosomes*. Chromosomes are strands of deoxyribonucleic acid (DNA) molecules present in the nuclei of the cells. A chromosome is divided up into a number of subparts called *genes* that are encoded with specific traits such as hair color, height, and intellect. Each specific gene (like the one for blood type) is situated in the same location on associated chromosomes in other beings of the same species. Small variations in a gene are called *alleles*. An allele will flavor a gene to create a slight variation of a specific characteristic. For example, in differing people a gene that specifies the blood group A may present as an allele for A+, and in another person an allele for A-. Chromosomes come in pairs, and each cell in the human body contains 23 of these pairs (46 chromosomes in total), with the exception of sperm and ova which only contain half as much. The first 22 pairs of human chromosomes are the same for both males and females, and it is the 23rd pair that determines a person's sex. At conception, when a sperm and ova meet, each containing half of their parent's chromosomes, a new organism is created. The meeting chromosomes merge to create new pairs. There are 8,388,608 possible recombinations of the 23 pairs of chromosomes with 70,368,744,000,000 gene combinations [Lefton94].

Evolutionary computing simulates the combining of chromosomes through reproduction to produce offspring. Each gene in a digital chromosome represents a binary value or basic functional process. A population is created with anywhere from one hundred to many thousands of individual organisms, where each individual is represented usually by a single chromosome. The number of genes in the organism will depend on its application. The population is put through its paces in a testing environment in which the organism must perform. At the end of the test, each organism is evaluated on how well it performed. The level of performance is measured by a fitness test. This test might be based on how fast the organism completed a certain task, how many weapons it has accumulated, or how many human players it has defeated in a game. The test can be whatever the programmer deems is a best judgment of a fit organism. Once the test is complete, the failures get killed off and the best organisms remain.[3]

These organism are then bred together to create new organisms which make up a new second generation population. Once breeding is complete, the first generation organisms are discarded and the new generation is put through its paces before being tested and bred. The process continues until an optimal population has been bred. This is a population that has found an optimal solution measured by the fitness test. It also comes at a point where further breeding of populations does not improve the population's performance by much, if at all.

There are several different methods that can be used to achieve evolutionary computing. These methods all work according to the process previously described. They are *evolution strategies*, *genetic programming*, and *genetic algorithms*. Evolution strategies simulate the natural evolution process to solve technical optimization problems. They are designed to replace an engineer's intuition by making random changes in experimental parameters to find an optimal design that might otherwise not be considered. For example, imagine the design for a new aircraft being put through its paces in a wind tunnel. To modify the aerodynamic properties of the aircraft, designers make continuous and often laboriously small changes to the design to find the optimal shape. The designer's task of making changes to the shape of the aircraft can be replaced with an evolution strategy. The idea behind genetic programming is to have computer programs breed better computer programs. In short, a selection of programs is used to solve a problem. The programs that compete the best are bred together to come up with a new and improved program. The idea behind all evolutionary programming methods is the process of natural selection and evolution.

The Offspring (*TNG#164*)

A chromosome in a genetic algorithm is represented by a string of symbols. Each chromosome is divided into a number of genes made up of one or more of the numbers. The numbers are usually binary; however, they need not be restricted to such. An outline of the genetic algorithm process follows, implementing a simple example for illustration purposes.

Step One: Create a Population and Determine Fitness

A genetic algorithm begins by specifying the length of a chromosome and the size of the population. A 4-bit chromosome would look like the one shown in Figure 8.1.

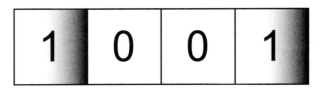

FIGURE 8.1   A 4-bit binary string for a digital chromosome.

Next, each individual in the population has its genes (the 1s and 0s) randomly assigned, as shown in Table 8.1. As previously stated, a real population would have many more organisms present, however in this case we will keep it simple. In this example, let's assume our fitness function is a mathematical equation defined by

$$f(x) = 2x + x^3.$$

Given this function, the fitness of each organism can be determined using the decimal value represented by the binary value stored in the chromosome string. The decimal value is substituted into the fitness function in the place of x. The result is a fitness value, as shown in Table 8.1. Next, the total fitness of the population is found by summing the fitness values of each organism and used to find an individual's fitness ratio. The fitness ratio is the individual's fitness divided by the population's total fitness. The fitness ratios for the organisms in the current example are shown in the last column of Table 8.1.

TABLE 8.1   The random assignment of gene values in a small population

Organism Id	Chromosome	Decimal value	Fitness	Fitness Ratio (%)
1	0011	2	12	0.6
2	1010	10	1020	49.7
3	1000	8	528	25.7
4	0111	7	357	17.4
5	0101	5	135	6.7

Step Two: The Mating of Chromosomes

There are a number of methods for pairing off chromosomes for mating selection. These include *statistical sampling* (also known as roulette wheel [Davis91]), *remainder sampling*, and *ranking* [Laramee02]. Statistical sampling takes a roulette wheel approach to selecting mating chromosomes (hence its other name). Each chromosome is allocated a portion of a circular wheel, the size of which represents its fitness ratio (as shown in Figure 8.2).

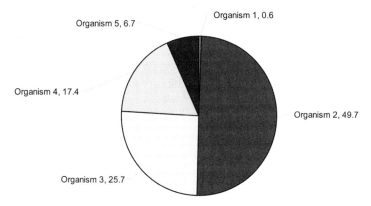

FIGURE 8.2   Statistic sampling roulette wheel.

A chromosome is selected for mating by conceptually spinning the wheel and picking the chromosome on which the wheel stops. This process can be simply programmed using the organism's fitness ratio as a probability of selection value. Organisms are mated until the new generation population is the same size as the old population. There is no reason why one organism cannot be selected a number of times. Remainder stochastic sampling determines if an organism is selected for mating based on the ratio of its fitness and the average population fitness. In the population from Table 8.1, the average fitness is 204, and Organism 1's ratio is equal to 0.06 and Organism 3's is 2.59. An organism is only mated if its ratio is greater than 1. If it is greater than 1, the organism is mated a number of times equal to the whole number part of the ratio. In this case that would

allow Organism 3 to mate 2 times. Finally, ranking mating, which is probably the simplest method, orders the organisms in descending order of
their fitness. Organisms near the top of the order are chosen for breeding
more times than ones lower down. A cut-off point may even be applied
where poorly performing organisms are culled from the population,
though these increase diversity, which can be valuable.

There are no hard and fast rules for selecting a mating strategy. In
[Laramee02] a new population is produced by cloning the top fittest 20
percent (this means copying the old organisms into the new population),
70 percent are mated according to their ranking, and 10 percent are newly
created organisms with random gene values.

So how is the chromosome of an offspring determined? When organisms are mated, the chromosomes of the parents will influence the chromosome of the child. This way, the fittest parents should pass on the cause
of their fitness to the child, though this is not always the case. Sometimes
the best parents can produce useless offspring and vice versa[4]. Any badly
created offspring will be phased out in future fitness tests, though. When
mated, the chromosomes of the parents may undergo a process called
crossover, typically with some probability. This process takes identically
sized segments out of each parent and swaps them to create two new chromosomes that are allocated to two new organisms. The crossover segment
is chosen through the generation of two random numbers that represent
the start and end gene locations of the crossover. For example, if Organism
2 and Organism 4 were chosen to mate, and the crossover segment was
from location 2 to 3, then the offspring's chromosomes would be 1110 and
0011, as shown in Figure 8.3.

Often a mating will result in clones of the parents. For example, if Organisms 2 and 3 were crossed over for the segment between 2 and 3 (the
middle 2 genes) then the result would be two children, each one a clone of
a parent. Crossover can also be achieved through coin tossing. In this case,
each of the genes in the parent's chromosomes is subject to a coin toss. If
heads comes up, the first parent's gene is added to the offspring's chromosome, and if tails comes up the gene is from the other.

In nature a rare event occurs in breeding called mutation. Here, an
apparently random gene change occurs. This may lead to improved fitness,
or, unfortunately, to a dramatically handicapped offspring. In evolutionary

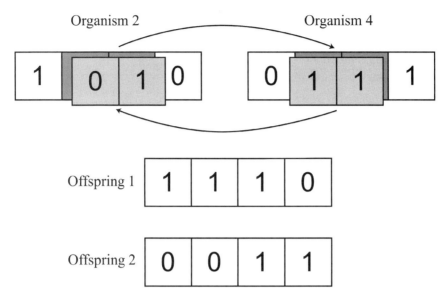

FIGURE 8.3   The crossover mating of two organisms and the resulting chromosomes.

computing, mutation can reintroduce possibly advantageous gene sequences that may have been lost through population culling. Mutation can be achieved by introducing new, randomly generated chromosomes into the population or taking new offspring and randomly flipping a gene or two. For example, an organism with a chromosome 0101 could be mutated by flipping the 3rd gene which would result in 0111.

Step Three: Introducing the New Population

The final step in a genetic algorithm is to replace the old population with the new one. It is important that the new population is the same size as the old one so they can be processed in the same way. Once the new population is in place, it is treated as the old one was and put through its paces and then tested for fitness.

The process is a cycle that continues creating and testing new populations until the fitness values converge at an optimal value. You can tell when this has occurred because there will be very little change in the fitness values from population to population. Just how optimal the fitness value is will be determined by the fitness evaluation function. In the case of the mathematical formulae used for the example given here, it is not possible to improve on the fitness function, because, in a sense, it is perfect. However, when working with a more complex scenario with artificial intelligences, the evaluation function may not be as clear cut and some experimentation may be needed to find the best balance.

We will examine an example genetic algorithm that the EMH might implement to find a cure for the Phage (*VOY:* "Phage"). We will assume the EMH has set up a computer simulation to evaluate the available treatments. Rather than trying the same treatment on every patient and evaluating the outcome, he could instead try a variety of treatments, assess their success, and then take the most successful ones and try combining the treatments to come up with a new set of treatments. Let's assume the EMH has five drugs that he would like to try in combination to come up with the best treatment. For simplicity we will call these Drug1, Drug2, Drug3, Drug4, and Drug5. The chromosomes for the experiment will represent the dose of each drug; therefore, the chromosome [0.1, 5.0, 0.0, 6.7, 1.2] would suggest 0.1cc of Drug1, 5cc of Drug2, etc. To begin the experiment, the EMH would have to create a population of chromosomes. He might set their values randomly, such as chromosome 1 = [0.2, 3.0, 5.9, 3.4, 0.0], chromosome 2 = [0.2, 0.9, 6.7, 4.5, 0.0], and so on. He might set these values for thousands of chromosomes. He could then apply the respective doses to the simulated patients. Once this is achieved, the EMH could measure the health of each patient. It could be assumed that the most healthy patients received a better combination and dosage of the drugs than the others. The EMH could then use the chromosomes of drug dosages from the most healthy patients and use them to breed a new set of chromosomes. When this is achieved, the simulation can begin again. If the EMH measures the average health of the patients for each chromosome generation, he might expect results similar to those shown in Figure 8.4.

In order for an artificial intelligence to execute a genetic algorithm it must be programmed with the ability to do so. The type of patient simulations we have just presented would have to be programmed into the EMH. The easiest way for this to be achieved is to have someone program the ability for him. However, what would happen if there was no one to write

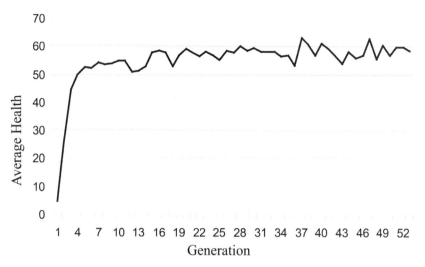

FIGURE 8.4   Average patient health versus chromosome generation.

a new subroutine for the EMH? It would be impossible for him to ever exceed his original programming. We could liken this to Data's ability to feel emotion. Without his emotion chip Data is incapable of feeling or expressing emotion, and he is also unable to reprogram himself to do so.

We therefore need to consider how an AI might reprogram itself. One answer is currently being explored in a field of research known as *genetic programming*.

BLOODLINES (*TNG#274*)

Genetic programming is all about getting a computer program to solve a problem without explicitly being programmed to do so. Like genetic algorithms, genetic programming also uses a process of natural selection to find the best solution to a problem. If you know anything about programming, you might think that some programming languages are quite simple. On the surface they might appear this way, but when you start trying to teach a computer how to use the language to write a new program for an unspecified problem, the task becomes overwhelming.

Let's start with a simple example of writing a program for a hologram to enable it to solve the Pythagorean Theorem. If you can remember your high school mathematics, you should recall that the theorem states that the square of the hypotenuse of a right angle triangle is equal to the sum of the squares of the other two sides, thus:

$$h = \sqrt{a^2 + b^2}.$$

You might look at this and think, "Hey, too easy." Of course it is quite elementary for you, who knows how to pick up a calculator and press the buttons, but consider that your hologram knows nothing about mathematics or the order in which to press the calculator buttons. It would be an elementary task to program it to solve the above equation; however, what if the equation changes? You would have to teach the hologram how to decipher an equation and then how to calculate the answer. Remember that it is not us that is reprogramming the hologram but itself. To add a line of code to the program that squares two numbers, adds them together, and then finds the square root is quite simple (for a programmer). In the C programming language it would look something like this

```
h = sqrt( pow(a,2) + pow(b,2) );
```

where sqrt is an operation that finds the square root and pow is an operation that finds the power of the first value to the second.

But you cannot just give the hologram this line of code and ask it to reprogram itself. Well, on second thought, maybe you could do something that resembled that. However, consider that you and your hologram are no longer together (because it has become lost in the delta quadrant) and it must learn Pythagoras' Theorem by itself. What you can do is teach it about programming code constructs and how to put code together, and then check if it is working. This is essentially how genetic programming works.

There are five steps you need to take to ensure your hologram was programmed ready to perform genetic programming when the need arises. The first step is to determine the number of inputs to consider. In the case of Pythagoras' Theorem, that would be two inputs: a and b. These are called *terminals*.

The second step is to provide the hologram with a set of *primitive* functions that it can use to write programs. For our hologram, that means a standard mathematical operation and some arithmetic operations. In other words, we need to teach the hologram where the square root (sqrt), addition (+), subtraction (–), division (/), and multiplication (*) buttons are on the calculator. However, you do not give it the order in which to press the buttons. Remember, you aren't going to be present when the hologram wants to learn Pythagoras' Theorem, and you didn't have the foresight to program it with it.

The terminals and primitives defined in the first two steps make up the building blocks the hologram can use to write programs.

The third set is to provide the hologram with a means of evaluating the output from its programs. The easiest way to do this is have it determine its error calculated as the difference between the result it calculates and the result it was after. This evaluation method is called the fitness function. It can differ from the one we have suggested. For example, it is more common that a result might need to be weighed against a number of desirable outcomes.

The next step is to decide on the parameters the hologram should use when it performs genetic programming. These are the same as for genetic algorithms. You will need to tell it the size of the population to work with and the maximum number of generations.

Finally, as the hologram writes and tries out various programs it will inevitably have successes and failures in coming up with a program whose output has the least error. When the maximum number of generations of the program have been run, the hologram may not have found an exact answer. Therefore, you need to program it to identify the program which is "best-so-far" and declare it as the result of its programming attempts. Once you have followed these five steps for programming your hologram, you can be assured it will be ready for genetic programming when the need arises.

Genetic programming proceeds along the same lines as genetic algorithms. The hologram would generate a population of programs, test the fitness of each, breed the most successful programs together, and discard the others. The process would continue until it comes up with a correct answer or it performs the maximum number of generations.

Let's have a look at a very simple example. Assume the hologram is given the inputs 3 and 4. According to Pythagoras' Theorem, we know that the answer will be 5. The hologram is also told that the answer is 5, but doesn't know how to work with 3 and 4 to come up with an answer. So it creates the initial population of programs shown in Table 8.2.

TABLE 8.2   An initial population of programs

Id	Program	Output	|Error|
1.	sqrt(a) + sqrt(b)	3.73	1.27
2.	(a + b) * 2	14.00	9.00
3.	sqrt(a + b) * 2	5.29	0.29
4.	(power(a,2) + power(b,2))/2	12.50	7.50

Obviously, for your hologram to have any success in coming up with an accurate program, it would need to generate far more initial programs than those shown in Table 8.2. Once the programs have been generated, the input given the values for *a* and *b* are substituted into the programs and output values are generated. These values are then compared with the desired output, in this case 5, to calculate an error. The error must be calculated on a range of inputs, because the correct answer can result from an incorrect equation.

The smaller the error the more fit the program. The error value is used to rank the programs and they can be placed into a breeding program. Breeding can occur in any of the same ways used for genetic algorithms. For example, you might throw away the bottom half of the programs and crossover the remaining. Crossover in programs can occur on any of the building block functions. Given the error values in Table 8.2, we would crossover programs 1 and 3. These would become the parent programs. Suppose we crossover parent 1 on the + and parent 3 on the *; we would get the children programs:

```
sqrt(a) * 2
sqrt(a + b) + sqrt(b)
2 * sqrt(b)
sqrt(a + b) + sqrt(a)
```

where the program parts of parent 1 are underlined. These would be the next generation of programs and could undertake the same fitness test to get ready for further breeding. Of course, using only one set of inputs and one desired output could lead the breeding program to come up with the program

        a + b - 2

which would produce an error of zero for our current set of input values (3 + 4 − 2 = 5). In this case, Pythagoras' Theorem would not have been learned. Because the theorem works for an infinite range of input values, these could be added to the terminal values, and more appropriate fitness tests could be carried out to hone in on a more correct program.

What we have just examined is genetic programming at its *simplest*. Imagine how much functionality would have to be programmed into Data or the EMH to allow them to write their own subroutines for just about anything! The task is purely mind-boggling.

JOURNEY'S END (*TNG#272*)

In this chapter we have but scratched at the surface of evolutionary computing research, though we will say that what you have read is an excellent introduction and should help you in a quest to further research these areas. In the next Part of this book, we will examine some highly debated areas of metaphysics that are only now being considered as critical inclusions in the study of AI. Could it be that they might hold the key to the artificial life forms of the *Star Trek* future?

REFERENCES

[Davis91] Davis, L., 1991, *The Handbook on Genetic Algorithms*, van Nostrand Reinhold, New York.

[Laramèe02] Laramèe, F. D., 2002, Genetic Algorithms: Evolving the Perfect Troll, *AI Programming Wisdom*, Rabin, S. (ed), Charles River Media, Hingham.

[Lefton94] Lefton, L. A., 1994, *Psychology*, Allwyn and Bacon, Needham Heights.

ENDNOTES

1. We make this distinction because an AI might be robotic, and therefore the program should be active while the whole device is active. Alternatively, if the AI is contained within a computer, it would be active only while its actual program is running regardless of whether the computer is turned on. Obviously an AI running on another computer system could not be active if the system is off.
2. In the sense that they are simpler than the usual programming language, but having said that, they can also be quite complex.
3. Just like Darwin's *survival of the fittest*.
4. Yes, we are still talking about genetic programming!

PART III

Soul

CHAPTER 9

Imagination and Creativity

CHAPTER OVERVIEW

We don't tend to associate imagination and creativity with the characteristics of a machine. In fact, because most people consider a machine to be programmed and incapable of free thought, they find it inconceivable that a machine could think up anything original. However this is not the case. In the same way that our thoughts can be seeded with the basic building blocks of an idea, so too can machines. But is the process we take to come up with a new concept different from that of a machine's because it is considered programmed? When Data paints a picture or solves an engineering problem, are his efforts awarded to Dr. Soong?

In this chapter we analyze the cognition of creativity and look at some examples both in today's world and in *Star Trek* where machines are pushing the boundaries of original thought and challenging their critics.

EYE OF THE BEHOLDER (*ENT#270*)

Creativity is a characteristic which makes humans unique. In *TNG*: "11001001," Geordi attempts to find out if Data is capable of creative thought by having him paint an impression of the Zylo eggs[1]. We also see Data's exploration of creativity through art in other episodes, such as *TNG*: "Hero Worship," *TNG*: "Tin Man," and *TNG*: "Birthright."

Data isn't the first artificial being to explore his artistic abilities. In 1973, Harold Cohen (a painter become AI researcher) conceived AARON, a computer program capable of autonomously generating drawings. AARON is programmed with two types of knowledge: knowledge about world objects and knowledge about visual representation. Given these, AARON is able to produce original works of art containing posed animals (including people) and plants in a geographical space (the current extent of his database of world objects).

AARON builds its image starting with a stick figure, whether it is of a plant or a person. The program has knowledge about legal postures, regular gestures, and proportional dimensions. Given this, the program can calculate a scene and visually represent it. The stick figure is used as a basis for the final image, which is constructed by bulking out the figure and then coloring it. An image created by AARON is shown in Figure 9.1.

FIGURE 9.1   AARON's interpretation of a plant and a human figure.

The works by AARON are indeed remarkable and, at present, unique, due to the millions of decisions the program makes each time it draws. This brings up the question of utter uniqueness. If AARON were allowed to run long enough, would it create the exact same image a second time [McCorduck91]? Although the likelihood of such an event occurring is very remote and might not happen within one's lifetime, it does still demonstrate AARON's programmatic behavior.

But is AARON being creative? And is it possible for an artificial being, such as Data, to possess such ability?

Dramatis Personae (*DSN#418*)

A forward thinker in metaphysics, Arthur Koestler, described creativity as the mental conjunction of two as yet unrelated and sometimes opposing ideas. He called this *bisociation* [Koestler64]. Interestingly enough F. Scott Fitzgerald thought the ability to have two unrelated thoughts at the same time to be a sign of intelligence. He stated *the test of a first-rate intelligence is the ability to hold two opposed ideas in mind at the same time and still retain the ability to function.* We might assume from this that in order to be creative, to have the two thoughts needed for bisociation, we first need to be intelligent.

Creativity being the product of an intelligent mind is not limited to artistic endeavors, but also to scientific ones. There are some famous examples of creativity stemming from bisociation. Edgar Allen Poe, the great writer of dark poetic fiction (e.g. *The Raven*), used to formulate his creative stories by sticking a pin into a dictionary three times and using the skewered words as the basis, then forcing a story idea which intertwined the trio (trisociation). Watson and Crick, the founders of the DNA double-helix, discovered the structure through bisociation of their work with a colleague's work on protein structures and the invention of microcomputing by Maurice Wilkes, which itself came about from the combination of the concept of programming and a circuit structure called a diode matrix. And what about the invention of the printing press? Gutenberg struggled for many years to devise a way to cast letter-types into an even imprint on paper until he visited a winery and studied a wine press.

Koestler [Koestler67] believes that everyday routine thought is comparable to playing a game such as chess. The rules are fixed and, although an arduous task, all possible future states of the game can be determined. For an AI, among whatever abilities it is programmed with will be the ones that it needs on a daily basis to achieve its goals. On the other hand, what if the rules or the environment change? How does the AI cope with the changes? Of course it must adapt. But this is a huge leap for a programmed being. Neural networks and genetic algorithms are capable of some adaptation, but only within the realm for which they have been programmed. For example, an AI might be programmed with a genetic algorithm that allows it to learn its best defence strategy for escaping from a Borg cube; it might then be able to use this same algorithm to learn how to escape from a Kazon ship. Unfortunately, this type of adaptation does not require any huge leaps of creativity from the AI, because it is only reapplying what it knows to a differing situation. This same algorithm would completely fail if the AI was required to use it to, for instance, bake a Tarvokian pound cake (*TNG*: "The Game"). However, if the AI had a different algorithm that it used to bake cakes and it combined this algorithm with the escape algorithm to produce a plan that helped it escape from a Borg ship by poisoning the Borg with a Tarvokian pound cake, then this would be considered a creative solution. Two dissociated pieces of knowledge are being put together to form something new.

The EMH achieved this type of creativity in *VOY*: "Phage," when Neelix's lungs were removed and the EMH was able to replace them with a holographic pair of lungs. To do this he needed to merge two unrelated bodies of knowledge: Talaxian physiology and holographic engineering. His creative reasoning might have gone something like this:

> *Neelix needs new lungs.*
>
> *A solid holograph can be made to replicate objects in the real[2] world.*
>
> *Lungs are a real world object.*
>
> *Let's use a solid holograph to mold a new set of lungs for Neelix.*

This might sound like deductive reasoning and essentially it is. The difference is that an AI program might store knowledge that is reasoned about in different memory depending on its purpose. For example, the knowledge the doctor has about physiology could be contained in memory separate from holographic engineering. The reason for this is that the smaller the chunks of memory that need to be accessed to solve a problem, the less time the program will take to run. If the EMH was needed to treat a Klingon patient, then it might be reasonable to assume that the doctor's knowledge of opera was irrelevant. Searching for a treatment to a Klingon flu in an opera database would be a futile attempt and take up the EMH's reasoning time. In short, what we are trying to say is that the more knowledge there is to search through, the longer the problem solving task will take. It also prevents the EMH from coming up with reasoning patterns such as

> *The Klingon flu requires a treatment for over-aggressiveness.*
>
> *Klingon opera calms the nerves.*
>
> *Klingon opera might be a treatment for the Klingon flu.*

Allowing an AI to have multiple knowledge bases with means to integrate the knowledge among them may well harbor the key to creative computer processing. However, one serious problem, known as *combinatorial explosion*, can occur when knowledge is allowed to be combined with other knowledge in an unlimited fashion. Let's take the EMH attempting to find a replacement for Neelix's lungs. His reasoning might have him considering the fact that Neelix needs a replacement and therefore present three options:

■   a lung transplant
■   replicating replacement lungs
■   creating artificial lungs.

At this point, for one problem, the EMH now has three solutions. Taking the first option, the EMH has to consider a further problem: which crew member will donate a lung. Assuming there are 150^3 crew members to choose from, the EMH now has 152 solutions: a transplant from one of 150 people, replicated lungs, or artificial lungs. Assuming there is only one way to replicate the lungs, we next consider creating artificial lungs. Ways of doing this might vary from papier maché to three-dimensional holography. Each of these adds to the number of possible solutions the EMH can choose from. This is but a small subset of the EMH's knowledge, yet he still might have come up with 200 or more ways to treat Neelix. The more knowledge gets combined in a creative manner, the more thoughts the EMH can have, and thus, ***BOOM***, combinatorial explosion.

CHILD'S PLAY (*VOY#239*)

The type of creative combining that we have just discussed inherently occurs in the breeding process in evolutionary computing we examined in the previous chapter. It might be that we see a creative process evolving through the use of genetic programming at work in *TNG*: "Encounter at Farpoint," when Commander William Riker first encounters Data while searching through a holographic rain forest on the Holodeck looking for the android. He finds Data leaning up against a tree attempting to whistle the tune *Pop Goes the Weasel*. Data can't get the ending of the tune correct. Riker announces his presence by whistling the correct ending. Data responds, "Marvellous, how easily humans do that." It is difficult to miss Data's look of wonderment. Later in the episode we learn that Data is capable of perfect audio capture and playback when he is asked by Captain Picard to keep a record of the court proceedings when Q has the human race on trial. Data is asked to read back something Q previously said, and Data responds by repeating Q word for word, in Q's exact voice. Even today's computers are capable of this. Knowing this, why would it be so difficult for Data to reproduce *Pop Goes the Weasel*? We might assume that Data wants to produce the tune on his own, not play back some recording. Therefore, given Data's ability to purse his lips and push air through them to make a whistling noise, he now has the task of producing the correct notes and putting them in the correct order.

One example of the use of genetic programming in producing music is that of the GP-Music System [Johanson98], which evolves short musical sequences. The terminals for the system are a series of notes and chords, and the primitive functions include operations such as playing two different notes in sequence, playing the same note twice, adding a rest after a note, and changing the octave. The fitness tests for this system are performed by human listeners who rate the tunes the system produces subjectively.

In the case of Data attempting to learn *Pop Goes the Weasel*, it might be that he has a recording of the tune stored in his memory and uses this as the fitness function for comparing the notes that he is able to produce by whistling. The same process might be used by the EMH in learning to sing opera. He, like Data, is programmed with vocal sub-processes that allow him to vocalize words. Using this programming, which would include terminals of words with different pitches, vibratos, volumes, etc., the EMH would use an actual opera recording as the fitness test. We can conclude that if the EMH and Data use actual recordings of a single piece of music or song to compare the fitness of their own performances, then eventually, through training, their performances will come to resemble the recording exactly.

In *TNG*: "The Defector," Data attempts to learn more about the human condition by acting out Shakespeare's *Henry V*. When Picard commends him on his performance, Data suggests he has improved because of his study of the performances of other classical actors. Picard rebukes him, saying that he will not be able to understand humanity by imitating others, but only though his own original performance. We could argue with Picard on this point. If Data were imitating only one other actor we might say that his performance is unoriginal. However, as Data is being influenced by a number of other performances, he is using these as the fitness functions for his own performance. By combining these, he is coming up with something original. We will agree with Picard on the point that imitating the performance of one person, or a combination of other people, does not mean that a human level of understanding is achieved. For example, Data imitating a range of Shakespearian actors no more helps him to understand the human condition than the genetic programming of the GP-Music program is able to understand the soul of jazz.

FACETS (*DSN#471*)

Another theory on the creative process examines it in a top down fashion and attempts to alleviate the exhaustive searches of the previous given process. This particular theory comes not from pure psychology, as with the preceding, but from AI. It works by using previous knowledge to best match new situations and then proceeds to iron out any parts of the previous knowledge that don't quite fit. A very simple example of this is when Naomi Wildman[4] sees a Qomar (*VOY*: "Virtuoso") for the first time. Having only encountered Bajorians[5] before, the child may refer to the zebra as a horse. What the child has done is to assess the new situation and relate it back to some previous encounter that closely represents this one to help characterize what she is seeing. She might then ask, "Why is there a Bajorian planet in the delta quadrant?" in order to come to a resolution in the difference between what she is seeing and what she knows. This process is listed in [Schank95] thus:

1. Detect an anomaly
    1.1. Characterize the anomaly   *(Bajorians don't live in the DQ)*
    1.2. Develop a question which, when answered, will resolve the anomaly   *(Why are there Bajorians in the DQ?)*
2. Explain the anomaly
    2.1. Search for an explanation that satisfies the question
        (The Caretaker put them here.)
        (They are a Bajorian colony that set out over 200 years ago.)
        (They are not Bajorian.)
    2.2. Apply the explanation to generate an explanation
        (The Caretaker took the Bajorians and established a planet for them.)
        (These Bajorians are a colony.)
        (These beings are not Bajorian.)
    2.3. Test the new explanation
        (The Caretaker didn't create a planet for any other beings that he kidnapped from the alpha quadrant, so how likely is it that he did for the Bajorians?)
        (These Bajorians are far more technologically advanced [and shorter] than the Bajorians in the alpha quadrant. How likely is that?)
        (These creatures don't look exactly like Bajorians. Maybe they are not.)
3. Learn from the explanation
    3.1. Search for a similar expectation failure in memory
        3.1.1. If one exists, generate new knowledge based on the explanation
        3.1.2. If not, index the failed expectation using the explanation
            (It is ok for aliens to look like each other but not be the same)
            (Aliens in the DQ that look like ones from the AQ are most likely not from the same race.)

This method helps to eliminate combinatorial explosion by first searching for an explanation to a problem by creatively applying existing knowledge to new situations, and then hashing out the bits that don't quite fit. In a way, it comes up with a simple solution rather than building up an elaborate web of explanations from scratch.

LEGACY (*TNG#180*)

Creativity, as with most metaphysical aspects of human behavior, is viewed in the AI community in a different light than that by the general public. While society sees creativity as an illustrious process, something beyond normal everyday thinking, and a gift endowed on a privileged few, creativity in a computer program tends to stem from normal cognitive processing, something ingrained in all our thinking processes without which we would be simple automatons (or possibly, not even that!).

What we hope this chapter does is to make you think about the computational process of creativity and how this characteristic can become analytical to the point that it is inserted into the programming of artificial beings to help them become capable of original thought.

REFERENCES

[Koestler64] Koestler, A., 1964, *The Act of Creation*, Penguin Books Ltd., London.

[Koestler67] Koestler, A., 1967, *The Ghost in the Machine*, Penguin Books Ltd., London.

[McCorduck91] McCorduck, P., 1991, *AARON's Code: Meta-Art, Artificial Intelligence, and the Work of Harold Cohen*, W.H. Freeman and Company, New York.

[Schank95] Schank, R. C. & Cleary, C., (1995) Making Machines Creative. In: S. Smith, T. B. Ward & R. A. Finke (eds) *The Creative Cognition Approach*. MIT Press. 229–247.

[Taylor04] Taylor, J. & Mazlack, L., 2004, Humorous Word Play Recognition, *International Conference on Systems, Man and Cybernetics Proceedings*, October 10–13, 2004, The Hague, The Netherlands.

ENDNOTES

1. An alien life form.
2. The *real Star Trek* world.

3. On stardate 48975.1 *Voyager* has 152 crew members. Neelix and the EMH can't donate. This leaves 150 possible candidates.
4. The first and only child born on *Voyager*.
5. Bajorians and Qomar share a similar ridged nose bridge, though the Qomar's is slightly higher on the forehead.

CHAPTER 10

Humor

CHAPTER OVERVIEW

Throughout his existence Data continually has the goal to become more human. Even with his superior abilities he still desires to possess more human characteristics. Data refers to these things as elements of *the human equation*. In particular Data is concerned with the concepts of humor and emotion. The EMH, on the other hand, seems to inherently have all these elements wrapped up. Obviously Dr. Zimmerman had a better grasp on the nature of humanity than Dr. Soong.

The aim of this chapter is to examine another of the elements of human nature that make humans uniquely human and act very different from everyday AI as we currently know it: humor.

RIDDLES (*VOY#227*)

In *TNG*: "Code of Honor," we see Data's first demonstrated frustrations with the nature of humanity. He visits Geordi, who is shaving with an inaccurate shaving device. Data asks him why he doesn't use a shaver with a perfect cut, and Geordi informs him that too many things are perfect and that humans don't tend to alway enjoy perfect efficiency[1]. Data notes that things always come back to *the human equation*. We assume this to indicate that Geordi and Data have had many such metaphysical discussions in the past. Then Geordi asks Data how he is going with his analysis of *the human equation*, and Data responds, "Constantly" with a particular reference to humor. He recites a joke about a man asking for a pound of *kiddelies* at a butcher's. The butcher tries to correct the man, suggesting that he wants *kidneys*. The punch line has the man responding, "I asked for kiddelies, diddle I." Geordi shakes his head in disgust, advising Data that the joke is too old and that he didn't tell it properly. Data then asks Geordi the big question, "How do you know when something is funny?" Unfortunately Geordi is not very forthcoming. He tells Data that *funny* is not something that is explainable. Data suggests that his failure to make Geordi laugh might be Geordi's fault and not his own. He is even further confused by the nature of humor when he succeeds in making Geordi laugh when his tongue slips and he announces, "includdeling the kiddelies I have told 662 jokes. . . ." To Geordi's hysterics he proclaims, "I did not mean it as a joke."

Data's confusion on the nature of humor mounts further when a charming ship's captain named Okona boards the *Enterprise* in *TNG*: "The Outrageous Okona." Okona points out that Data's inability to find things funny is a serious obstacle in Data's quest to become more human. This, of course, isn't the first time that Data considers the subject of humor, nor is it the last. As we watch Data on his pursuit towards humanness, the topic of humor is emphasized again and again. In this particular episode, Data is lead to the Holodeck in an attempt to define *funny*. Unfortunately, the holographic stand-up comedian he calls upon defines funny as something that makes you laugh. A rather vague definition because Data might have concluded that a particular subroutine inserted into his programming could make him laugh, or, more accurately, simulate laughter. When Data asks the stand-up to show him what is funny, the character begins with a Jerry Lewis impersonation. After Data attempts to replicate the character's impersonation, he states, "So wearing funny teeth and jumping around like an idiot is considered funny."

In *TNG*: "The Naked Now," Data hears a limerick recited by some of the crew members. In his struggle to understand its humor, he begins narrating it to Captain Picard, with Worf listening. He starts, "There was a young lady from Venus, whose body was shaped like a . . ." Picard cuts him off. When Data asks Worf if he said something wrong, Worf responds that he doesn't understand human humor either.

THE BATTLE (*TNG#110*)

The actual fact of the matter is that not even we as humans totally understand humor, and if we expect it to be replicated in AI, we need to fully analyze it. The best place to start, however, is with the organ that recognizes humor, the brain. When we hear a joke, brain activation follows a fairly conventional sequence involving the areas of the brain used for language processing and ambiguity resolution. This is the first stage in humor recognition and is called cognitive processing. The great thing about cognitive processing is that it is very analytical and quantifiable and easily (we use this term loosely) converted into a computer program. We will take particular advantage of this characteristic of humor recognition in a moment.

Following the cognitive processing, a variety of other brain areas become active. These include the parts linked with addiction and emotion.

From research into the physiological effect of humor, neuroscientists have discovered the following:

1. The cognitive and emotional aspects of jokes activate the language processing, incentive, and emotion parts of the brain,
2. the brain processes jokes cognitively and then emotionally, and
3. some jokes work on the ambiguity resolution parts of the brain.

The theories on humor and the academic categorizations of humor are quite extensive. They range from accidental humor, when, for example, someone trips or fumbles or says something unexpected, to deceitful humor, for instance, a plastic ice cube complete with fly placed in someone's glass, to riddles. The earliest theory on humor was devised by none other than the famous psychologist Freud [Freud28]. As you would expect, his theory revolves around sex and aggressiveness! He concluded that there were two types of jokes: *innocent*, which would elicit little more than a smile, and *tendentious*, which could cause rolling-around-on-the-floor laughter.

Another theory used in AI applications is Raskin's Semantic Script-based Theory of Humor [Raskin85]. Put simply, Raskin's theory suggests that a joke is composed of two scripts and these scripts overlap or interact such that the meaning of one script opposes the other. For example,

The first thing that strikes a stranger in New York is a big car.

As you can see, the scripts aren't necessarily contained in separate sentences. When first reading the joke, you take the meaning of *strike* to be similar to *surprise*. However, after reading *a big car*, it dawns on you that *strike* can also mean *hit*. Thus, you get this opposing set of meanings in your mind and as you figure out the ambiguity you find it funny. Having reconciled the scripts in the joke, it isn't as funny the next time you read it. This type of joke relies on wordplay. This is similar to the division in deductive reasoning which we examined in Chapter 7. For example, in *VOY*: "Riddles," Tuvok is trying to determine how a fictitious ensign could survive on a desolate planet with nothing but a calendar. When Neelix suggests that the ensign could eat the dates from the calendar, we experience this wordplay effect in creating humor. Later in the episode Tuvok points out that the ensign could also eat the Sundays. Although the wordplay in this case means swapping *sundae* for *Sunday*, in a verbal joke, spelling can be irrelevant.

Another type of joke that uses wordplay is the *knock knock joke* (KKJ). A KKJ is a lot more structured than a free format joke and therefore more ideal to analyze and recreate in a computer program. Let's examine a KKJ structured thus[Taylor04]:

1. "Knock, Knock"
2. "Who's there?"
3. any phrase
4. Line 3 followed by "who?"
5. One or more sentences containing one of the following:
   - Line 3
   - A wordplay on Line 3
   - A meaningful response to Line 4

For example:

Knock Knock
Who's there?
Water.
Water who?
Water you doing?

In a KKJ the wordplay occurs on the word or phrase in line 3. This makes it very easy for a computer program to determine which words it should be playing. The wordplay in the preceding joke occurs on the word *water,* taking advantage of the fact that *what are* sounds like *water.* This type of word or phrase substitution is quite easy for a human to achieve, but what about a computer? One method, outlined in [Taylor04], takes the keyword (in this case *water*) and runs it through an algorithm that comes up with other words that sound similar. For example, it might come up with *watel, watar, whatare,* etc. It then takes these words and determines if a proper phrase can be constructed. In this case, *whatare* can become *what are.* Next the program needs to complete the sentence for line 5. All the program has to do is find the most common sequence of words that follow *what are* and, *hey presto*, we have a punchline.

Data uses the same principles for wordplay in *STVII: Generations*. In this movie, Data makes a false deduction, assuming that because the crew find it funny that Worf lands over the side of a holographic ship into the water, that it might also be funny if he pushed Dr. Crusher over the side. Not getting the reaction he was expecting (instead getting angry and perplexed glares from the crew), he decides his emotion chip should be permanently installed. When the emotion chip overloads, Data starts cracking jokes left, right, and center. After he successfully opens a door with a magnetic lock, he jokes, "You could say I have a magnetic personality," playing on the word *magnetic*.

It is obvious that Data can recognize the wordplay in jokes. For example, Guinan says to him during an encounter, "You are a droid and I am a noid," where *a noid* is a play on *annoyed* and Guinan's intention that *noid* is short for humanoid. Data recognizes the wordplay after pondering over it for a while. However, he is puzzled as to why he does not find it funny. The point we are trying to make is that if Data can recognize a joke during cognitive methods, then the most probable way for this to make him laugh is to program him to do so.

At the end of the episode, *TNG*: "The Outrageous Okona," Guinan counsels Data, suggesting that being able to make people laugh is not the be-all and end-all of being human. Data sighs and says, "But there is nothing more uniquely human."

THE OUTRAGEOUS OKONA (*TNG#130*)

Having read this and Chapter 9 you may notice how closely humor is related to creativity. This means that although our ultimate goal in creating an artificial intelligence may not be to program one that can crack a joke, the very same analytical processes might be necessary to enhance its learning and thinking processes. Of course, if, as Data suspects, humor is the solution to the human equation, should we by accident produce the first artificial comedian, we might conclude that we have succeeded in the penultimate goal of AI.

REFERENCES

[Freud28] Freud, S., Humour, *International Journal of Psychoanalysis* 9 (1928): 1–6.

[Raskin85] Raskin, V., 1985. *Semantic Mechanisms of Humor.* Dordrecht, Boston.

[Taylor04] Taylor, J. & Mazlack, L., 2004, Humorous Word Play Recognition, *International Conference on Systems, Man and Cybernetics Proceedings,* October 10–13, 2004, The Hague, The Netherlands.

ENDNOTE

1. A sentiment that would wholly be supported by Seven of Nine.

CHAPTER 11

Emotions

CHAPTER OVERVIEW

The aim of this chapter is to examine another element of human nature that Data previously struggled with on a daily basis until his evil twin brother Lore bestowed him with the ultimate gift: emotion. Several advocates of AI, such as Marvin Minsky and Rosalind Picard[1], agree that characteristics such as emotion are extremely important in creating real artificial intelligence. To this end, in this chapter we examine the concept of emotion.

HOPE AND FEAR (*VOY#194*)

All of the metaphysical concepts discussed in this section involve emotion. In fact, Marvin Minsky (an AI founder) suggests that the concept of emotion might be that which finally ties all of the efforts in AI together into a more complete model. We recognize the participation emotion has in the preceding sections, but what exactly is it?

Emotion presents itself as a non-concise term in many of the domains that boast an understanding of the topic. These range from neurology and psychology to artificial intelligence. The reason may be that the term is used to describe a large range of cognitive and physiological states in sentient beings.

Emotions are often referred to in the broad sense, to describe not only familiar feelings such as *happiness* and *sadness*, but also biological motivational urges such as *hunger* and *thirst*. Koestler summed up this general view, defining emotions as "... mental states accompanied by intense feelings and involving bodily changes of a widespread character" [Koestler67]. The degree of difficulty plaguing this subject matter is that a person rarely experiences a *pure* emotion. For example, feelings of *hunger* may be accompanied by feelings of *frustration*. However, there is a logical intuitive difference in defining *hunger* as an emotion and *frustration* as an emotion. Another general definition of emotion given by Lefton defines emotion as "... a subjective response (feeling), usually accompanied by a physiological change, that is interpreted by the individual, then readies the individual for some action that is associated with a change in behavior" [Lefton94]. This proposition recognizes the meeting of the minds that Freud predicts, and although this does not attempt to explicitly define an emotion, it meshes the logical theory that emotions are indeed physiologically produced in an individual and affect that individual psychologically.

Of course, this later stance is clear in the field of neuropsychology, where emotional behavior is explained as physiological and treated at this level with chemicals. For example, patients with severe depression can be successfully treated with medications containing serotonin (an essential neurotransmitter found in the brain and spinal cord) that replaces essential neuropeptides lacking in the brain. However, much research in generating psychological theories and models ignores the biological counterpart. For example, many reasoning, decision-making, belief, personality, and social behavior models have been developed in complete isolation of the physiological domain.

There exists a plethora of theories and models on emotions. Many of these have been conceived to explore different emotional concepts from different perspectives. Some theories were designed to explain the physiological generation and effects of emotion, some place an emphasis on the lower primal emotions that influence and generate motivational states, while others examine the discrete categorisation of emotional reactions and their antecedents.

BLISS (*VOY#209*)

According to Picard [Picard97], if computers are ever to exhibit or have emotions, they must be capable of synthesizing and generating them. Picard outlines five components present in a human emotional system, where all or subsets of these must be present, in an emotional computer system. These are 1) emotional behavior; 2) fast primary emotions; 3) cognitively generated emotions; 4) emotional experience: cognitive awareness, physiological awareness, and subjective feelings; and, 5) body-mind interactions.

Emotional Behavior

The area of emotional behavior refers to systems that display outward emotions. This does not necessarily mean the system has the means to internally process emotional responses as humans do, but nonetheless is capable of appearing emotional. Data (before the installation of his emotion chip) was capable of expressing emotions even though he could not internally generate them. For example, he could smile or show when he was puzzled. This type of behavior is for the total benefit of those around him in an HCI sense, because it only helps to strengthen bonds between him and those around him. It also provides others with insight as to what he is thinking and to assist in communication. When Data looks puzzled, it can be construed by others that their communication with him needs further clarification.

Fast Primary Emotions

The brain, in response to stimuli that evoke a survival mechanism, generates fast primary emotions. One such application of fast primary emotions in artificial beings would be to implement survival mechanisms where they could quickly react to protect themselves. This could include such things as getting out of the way of moving objects, ducking, the heightening of perceptual sensors, or renewing their power supply.

Another subset of these primary emotions is drives or motivational urges. These systems work by generating internal motivations that activate the goals of the AI. The ideas behind these systems are essentially the same. A timing mechanism or change in state of the being generates an urge that in turn triggers a goal.

Emotional Experience

An emotional experience is the ability of a machine to have an awareness of its emotional state. This awareness may be accompanied by changing physiological states (an example in humans being an increased heart beat) and may be generated by internal subjective feelings. These internal feelings, or *gut feelings,* are very difficult to implement in computers due to the fact that in humans they are produced biochemically.

When Data has his emotion chip installed in *STVII: Generations,* he begins to experience emotions. On a visit to Ten Forward, the social hub of the *Enterprise,* Guinan offers him a new drink from Forcas Three. At first he is unable to articulate the emotion the drink has generated within him. His face clearly shows disgust. Guinan suggests that it looks like he hates it. Data is so delighted to pinpoint his new emotion that he accepts more of the awful drink when next offered.

Emotions in humans act as gauges by which we can qualify our experiences. Bad emotional experiences often prevent us from placing ourselves in similar situations that might cause the feelings to return. In the preceding drink example, Data is able to express an emotion generated from a beverage that has a biological effect on his chemical analysis routines, but does not act on it. For humans, the drink might be poisonous, and therefore an awful taste could be enough to prevent them from drinking further.

Later in the movie, Data and Geordi are cornered on a science station by Professor Soran who threatens them with a weapon; Data's emotion chip goes into overdrive. He begins experiencing fear and lets it overwhelm his operating capacity. However, unlike the drink, the new emotions of fear and anxiety that he feels do indeed influence his behavior. A once strong, unwavering character, Data is reduced to a blubbering mess.

Body-Mind Interactions

This section refers to the influence that emotions have on the body and mental states of humans. The study of emotions from a neural basis is an active field of research. Emotions can influence the body's state and, in turn, the body's state can influence emotion. For example, if you feel happy you will smile, and research has discovered that, if you first smile, you will then feel happy.

Now the EMH is definitely an artificial being that wears his heart on his sleeve. From the moment he is activated he apparently has a chip on his shoulder and repeatedly gets irritated, impatient, and depressed. Dr. Lewis Zimmerman, the EMH's creator, obviously has a really good grasp on the programming of emotion[2]. We are not going to look at this programming here as it is currently beyond our abilities to write such a complex emotional program. However, because the EMH does experience emotional times when his emotions affect his programming and his programming affects his emotions, we thought it pertinent to have a look at a couple of these instances in this section.

In *VOY*: "Projections," the EMH finds himself activated with all crew members having evacuated *Voyager*. As the EMH tries to determine what has happened he begins noticing that he registers on medical instruments as having life signs. His program also malfunctions to the point that it causes him to experience physical pain and bleed, something for which he is not programmed. These unexpected glitches in his programming cause him to experience anxiety, anger, and confusion. Here we see the state of his programming creating emotional responses.

In *VOY*: "Latent Image," the EMH discovers that his memory of several past events has been deleted. In his attempts to discover the reasons, he uncovers a conspiracy against him in which the Captain intentionally deleted his memories to overcome a conflict in his programming. After much debate, the Captain agrees to restore the missing memories. The EMH ascertains that during an away mission, Harry Kim and Ensign Jetal were attacked such that they begin to experience massive synaptic failure. The EMH is faced with the decision of which crew member to save; he is the only one who can perform a successful operation and they are both in a critical condition. The EMH chooses to operate on Harry and, as a result, Ensign Jetal dies. As the EMH reflects on his actions he cannot come to terms with his decision to save Kim over Jetal just because he has a close friendship with Harry. As his emotions of remorse, confusion, and guilt overwhelm him, it causes a feedback loop in his programming, and he cannot escape the perpetual loop of trying to reason about his actions. In this case, we see the EMH's emotional responses affecting his programming.

Cognitively Generated Emotions

These emotions may be explained as the emotions that follow primary emotions. They are the emotions generated on appraisal of a stimulus. Over the past 15 years this categorical approach to the study of emotion has become prominent in psychology. Groups of theorists known as cognitive appraisal theorists have attempted to explain different emotional reactions by categorizing emotions based on evaluating the situations from which the emotions arose. The long-term interest in the classification of emotional experiences has traditionally only been defined in two dimensions: *pleasantness* and *arousal*. However, these appraisal dimensions were found to be inadequate in classifying the range of human emotional states and newer models arose using more complex appraisal dimensions including *responsibility*, *effort*, *certainty*, and *control*.

When Data tastes the horrible drink in Ten Forward, his programming begins to appraise the situation. It examines how the chemicals in the drink interact with his tastes and assesses that the taste is unpleasant. The emotion chip could then use this appraisal to generate in Data the appropriate emotional response.

DRIVE (*VOY#249*)

The human equation, what Data longs to understand and what the EMH apparently has mastered, is a combination of metaphysical characteristics of human behavior that, in the past, have defied explanation. Although the field of psychology is famous for theorizing about these qualities, it has not been until recently that the domain of AI has started to take them seriously.

Most importantly, it is discovering how elements such as humor, creativity, and emotion can best enhance the behaviors of an artificial being and figuring out how to incorporate these into such a logical mind.

REFERENCES

[Koestler67] Koestler, A. 1967, *The Ghost in the Machine*, Penguin Books Ltd., London.

[Lefton94] Lefton, L. A. 1994, *Psychology: Fifth Edition*, Allyn and Bacon, Boston.

[Picard97] Picard, R. 1997, *Affective Computing*, The MIT Press, London.

ENDNOTES

1. A researcher with a particularly enviable surname!
2. A shame he hasn't published his research in the past.

CHAPTER 12

How to Make Friends and Influence Humans

CHAPTER OVERVIEW

Having a personal relationship with your own computer is something that couldn't be further from your mind. However, some researchers think that it is an essential area to study. In brief, they say that if you like your computer then you will have a better working relationship. This relationship, however, is totally one-sided, as the attachment and feelings with which humans identify a relationship are not something reciprocated by the machine. In this chapter we ask, "What does an artificial intelligence have to do to fake a relationship, and does it really matter if it can't *feel* in the same way that we do?"

LOOKING FOR PAR'MACH IN ALL THE WRONG PLACES (*DSN#501*)

When we first sat down to write this section it was called *Love*, and the idea was to try and explain how Data and the EMH could fall in love. Indeed, we see this occur in the case of the EMH in *VOY*: "Lifesigns," when he falls for the Vidian scientist Dr. Danara Pel. His outward display of affection towards others is also evident in *VOY*: "Virtuoso," where he mistakes the interest in his operatic abilities from a Qomari woman named Tincoo for love, and in *VOY*: "Someone to Watch Over Me," where his deep feelings for Seven of Nine are revealed.

Data also encounters love but from a different perspective. In *TNG*: "The Naked Now," Data experiences a sexual encounter with Lieutenant Tasha Yar when the crew is intoxicated by an alien contaminant. We learn at this point that, when it comes to physical love, Data is fully functional and programmed in multiple techniques. The relationship is extremely brief and totally physical with no lasting psychological ramifications. Note, this isn't the type of relationship we are going to discuss in this section. What we are more interested in is the relationship Data has with Lieutenant Jenna D'Sora in *TNG*: "In Theory." In this episode Jenna, recently separated from her boyfriend, has a rebound relationship with Data. Although Data attempts to program himself to manage the intricacies of such a relationship, he fails in his attempt.

This brings us to the main topic of this section. How can we describe love from an analytical perspective with the aim of programming it into an artificial being? "Oh, now you are just getting silly," we're sure you're thinking. The idea of mechanical artificial beings being able to love may seem ridiculous. Although there are many cases in Star Trek when computers exhibit an unusual bond with others, it might be artificial on one side, but it is definitely real on the other. The very idea that you could find yourself in love with your computer is quite disturbing and many would just dismiss the idea. But some researchers are endeavouring to study the relationships people have between each other in order to recreate them between man and machine.

If you think about the relationships you have had in the past, undoubtedly there would be other people such as your mother, father, siblings, best friend at school, dog, cat, goldfish, etc. All these entities tend to be somewhat . . . alive? But think about some inanimate objects you have had relationships with such as a teddy bear, Legoland inhabitants, Cabbage Patch dolls, Quakebots, . . . your car. All of these objects possess the same characteristic of not being able to express or feel their relationship with you. In reality, the relationship is one sided. It's all in your head, as they say. Yet you make yourself believe they are capable of feeling and expressing the relationship in the same way as you.

Now imagine if one of these inanimate objects actually responded in a way you had been fantasizing about. Besides shocking your socks off, it would reinforce your beliefs about the nature of the relationship and possibly strengthen your bond with that object. Admit it or not, you probably have already established a relationship with your computer; especially if the thought of throwing it out of a tenth story window has ever crossed your mind. It might not be love, but it is a strong relational bond!

INTERFACE (*TNG#255*)

In a field called Human Computer Interaction (HCI), developers and researchers are especially interested in the relationships we have with computing devices. The more user-friendly the devices are, the more likely you are to continue using them. If you manage to come to an understanding with your computer, then your working together is much more productive. The question that remains is, how can you develop a meaningful relationship with a computer? To answer this, we need to examine human-to-human relationships.

A relationship can be defined as a bond that exists between beings having interactions with each other. A relationship is such that participant's behaviors are interdependent, in that the actions of one influence the state of the other [Kelly83]. In addition, there are no particular patterns of interaction between relationships, but rather the interactions in a relationship are unique for each individual relationship. In our culture there are often provisions that friends offer each other; these include a sense of belonging, emotional stability, self-expression, physical and emotional support, and personal validation [Duck91].

As should be clear by now, if you are going to program a computer to behave like a human, then you need to have a model of how a human behaves. There are probably as many theories and models on relationships as there are relationships themselves. The previous definition of a relationship between two participants is called a dyadic model. Others include *economic models*, where there is a cost versus benefit analysis in social exchanges; *dimensional models*, where characteristics of relationships (such as power, hostility, formality, and intensity) are measured and compared against each other; and *stage models*, where relationships are broken into phases (e.g. initial rapport, mutual self-revelation, mutual dependency, and need fulfillment) [Reiss60].

The work currently being performed in HCI with respect to relationships is in the area of strategic relationships, where the computer attempts to establish a bond of trust with the user in order to increase acceptability and aid in usability and interaction. When we first see the EMH activated in *VOY*: "Caretaker" and closely following episodes, the crew have very little regard for the hologram. Although he, in his own words, is the embodiment of modern medicine (*VOY*: "Parallax") with knowledge from 2000 medical sources and the expertise of 47 practitioners, the crew are still wary of him. As it is today, people can acknowledge that computers can assist them and do some tasks better than they can, but they still do not trust them completely. The relationships that develop between the EMH and crewmembers follow a typical relationship management regime. In the beginning, relationships form simply from regular interactions, more or less like the relationship you have with your mobile phone. It takes no extra effort or metaphysical characteristic on the side of the phone. It is all in your head. And this is okay, until the relationship gets boring and you buy a new phone. The crew of *Voyager* do not have this option when it comes to the EMH. In fact, for the EMH to succeed in its purpose, it needs explicit trust from the crew at the same level you would have with a human doctor trying to save your life. It becomes not only a question of convincing the crew to trust the EMH, but building the correct mechanisms into his program to allow him to change the nature of his relationships.

Ways in which HCI researchers see that computers can contribute to the dynamics of the relationship they have with their users are similar to those used between humans. One way to change the nature of an existing relationship is to perform new activities together. This is usually achieved through a negotiation process. The EMH achieves this with Seven of Nine by exploring activities with her beyond the usual doctor-patient interactions, such as singing and self-improvement lessons.

Another way to improve a relationship is to analyze it and talk about its nature. Soon after the EMH is activated, the Captain is inundated with complaints about his attitude (*VOY*: "Eye of the Needle"). When Kes visits her to discuss the crew's rudeness towards the EMH, the Captain reveals the other side of the story. After some convincing, the Captain decides not to reprogram the EMH to better his attitude, but decides to change the nature of her relationship with him. What transpires is a heightened respect for the EMH, and, in turn, he modifies his attitude towards his patients and improves his bedside manner.

In addition, a further important aspect in relationship maintenance is empathy, or the ability to understand another's emotions. Empathy requires an individual to have experienced or be able to recreate in their mind a similar set of circumstances to understand the emotional reactions of another. Indeed, in *VOY*: "Tattoo," the EMH programs himself with the 29-hour Levodian flu to gain a better insight into his patients' suffering. Not convinced that the EMH will learn from an experience that he knows will end at a specific time, Kes adds a few extra hours to the program during which the EMH experiences true anxiety and a plethora of other emotions. In the end, the experience enhances the EMH's ability to express empathy. This, in turn, modifies his attitude when dealing with patients, and this change in behavior is reciprocated.

THE PERFECT MATE (*TNG#221*)

When it comes down to it, it is highly unlikely that artificial beings will ever be advanced enough to experience love at any level in the same way as humans. The best we could hope for is that they can be programmed to fake it. By this we mean that they exhibit all the outward behaviors applicable in relationships to the point that they fool the other. We are not suggesting that this faking of love is for some ultimate evil purpose where the AI could turn on their partner at any moment (although this would not be out of the question), but that the intentions of the programmers are sincere in allowing their AIs to form lasting bonds with flesh and blood beings.

In *VOY*: "Fair Haven," Tom Paris recreates a small Irish village complete with villagers on the Holodeck. One of the characters, Michael Sullivan, owns and runs the village pub. When Captain Kathryn Janeway first visits the pub in search of some of her crew and to assess the Holodeck program her first encounter is with the Sullivan character. Now if you aren't familiar with the nature of the Holodeck[1], the characters therein are indistinguishable from flesh and blood people. Janeway exchanges a few quips with the publican and a mutual "their eyes met across a crowded room"-type stare. Although we know from past experience with the EMH that Janeway has strong opinions about the nature of holograms (in particular their personhood), from this moment onward we watch the Captain form a lasting relationship with the Sullivan hologram.

On their next encounter, Janeway enters the pub after hours to find Sullivan closing up for the evening. After some initial rapport the hologram challenges Janeway to a game of ring toss. Unable to turn down any challenge, Janeway accepts. At the end of the evening, after a number of challenges, Sullivan reveals to Janeway that it has been nice to make a new friend and that she has a nice way about her. There is an interesting point we will make here. A study in human-computer relationships found that people like their computer more when the computers flatter them [Reeves96] just as Sullivan did Janeway.

The same study also revealed that the human-computer relationship was stronger when the computers matched their user's personality. This same observation is true in human-human relationships. The only difference is that it is difficult for two individuals to align their personalities.

What usually occurs is that the relationship does not develop. In the case of computers, though, they are programmed by humans and therefore able to be reconfigured to fit their user's requirements. Before Janeway continues with her relationship with Sullivan, she admits that she found him interesting and for a while forgot he was a hologram. Her next set of actions clearly demonstrates a human's ability to control the human-computer relationship.

When we next see Janeway she is walking the corridors of *Voyager* towards the holographic research lab. She admits that she and the current Sullivan are not truly compatible because Paris didn't have her in mind when he programmed the character. However, that really isn't a problem when you know how to program! Janeway's first modification to Sullivan is to increase his (simulated) intelligence level by giving him the education of a 19th century, 3rd year literary student. Next she wants him to be more provocative, outspoken, and curious. She also adjusts his physical parameters, making him three centimetres taller and neatening his facial hair. Before saving his program back to the Holodeck, she performs some final fine-tuning. Janeway accesses the character's interpersonal subroutines and...deletes the wife!

After a while the relationship between Sullivan and Janeway becomes physical.[2] It is at this point that Janeway becomes disillusioned with the relationship. On a picnic when Sullivan falls asleep under a tree, Janeway is just about to modify his snoring programmatically, when it hits her that the whole relationship is a farce. Which brings us to a couple of questions we will raise, but not answer here. Can a true relationship exist where one participant fully controls the other? Is there an attraction factor in the inability to fully control another? Personalities are complex, matching them even more so; what massive feat of programming is required to create personalized computer relationships?

BLOOD FEVER (*VOY#157*)

As we have shown, if not now, in the very near future the state of human-computer relationships as we know it will change. We don't envisage man/machine matrimonial relationships such as those portrayed in *Star Trek*, but we are beginning to see computers programmed to match our personalities. Whether or not the artificial being is experiencing the relationship is not important. What is important is that it can make us believe that it does.

This chapter concludes our look at the human equation, what Data longs to understand and what the EMH apparently has mastered, as a combination of metaphysical characteristics of human behavior that in the past have defied explanation. Although the field of psychology is famous for theorising about these qualities, it has not been until recently that the domain of AI has started to take them seriously. Most importantly, it is discovering how elements such as humor, creativity, and emotion can best enhance the behaviors of an artificial being, and figuring out how to incorporate these into such a logical mind.

REFERENCES

[Duck91] Duck, S. 1991. *Understanding Relationships*. New York, Guilford Press.

[Kelly83] Kelley, H. 1983. Epilogue: An essential science. *Close Relationships*. H. Kelley, A. Berscheid, J. Christensenet al. New York, Freeman: 486–503.

[Reeves96] Reeves, B. and C. Nass 1996. *The Media Equation*. Cambridge University Press, Cambridge.

[Reiss60] Reiss, I. L. 1960, Toward a Sociology of the heterosexual love relationships, *Marriage and Family Living*, 22:139–145.

ENDNOTES

1. Shame on you!
2. We are only speculating about this as we don't see it, though they do kiss passionately.

Epilogue

CHAPTER 13

Intelligence and Fooling the Turing Testers

CHAPTER OVERVIEW

As we have witnessed throughout this book, the AI in Star Trek could indeed be said to have intelligence. However, is it true that intelligence by its very definition (in Chapter 1) would allow artificial beings in possession of it to fool an onlooker to thinking they were flesh and blood? One of the ultimate challenges that exists in AI today is just that: to create an artificial being that is so much like a real human that it can fool an actual human into thinking it also is human.

Many of the artificial beings in *Star Trek*, including Data, the EMH, and the Holodeck characters, are often mistaken by the lay person for true biological beings, but is it their real intelligence that causes this perception or something else? In this chapter we will examine this very issue.

OBSESSION (*TOS#047*)

In 1950, mathematician Alan Turing asked the question, "Can machines think?" [Turing50]. He went on to demonstrate that such a question was quite ambiguous because it required definition of the words *machine* and *think*. His hesitancy to answer this question started a philosophical debate on the topic of thinking machines, as you will soon come to appreciate. Instead he proposed what later came to be known as the Turing Test. During this test, an artificial device and a human being are interrogated by means of a natural language exchange. The human interrogator does not know which participant is a machine and which is a person. The test is conducted under conditions similar to an Internet chat room, where participants cannot see each other, they can only interact via a textual message repartee. If, after a series of cognitive tasks, the interrogator cannot identify the machine from the human, the machine passes the test. In order to achieve such a level of deception, the computer would have to possess skills in natural language processing[1], storage of previously acquired information, and the abilities to answer questions, draw conclusions, adapt, and extrapolate information. Turing's original test avoids physical contact between both participants, as physical embodiment is not a prerequisite for intelligence. However, with advances in technology and further thinking, the Turing

Test has been updated to become the *Total Turing Test*. Mechanical participants in this test, while still not in physical contact with the interrogator, must also possess the abilities of visual recognition and object manipulation and relocation.

It is possible the Turing Test might tell us little about the actual thinking processes of a machine and more about its ability to mimic human behavior and fool others. If a machine passes the Turing Test, according to Turing, it would have exhibited intelligent behavior and be capable of achieving human-level performance in all kinds of thinking tasks. However, imagine you have to create a computer program that could pass the Turing Test. This is what some die-hard AI programmers attempt each year, competing for $2000 and a bronze medal in the Loebner Prize (*www.loebner.net*). Interaction with the programs is via text-based conversation. Judges for the prize give points to the programs for how human they seem. If you were writing such a program, would you be trying to fool the judges or to actually create a thinking machine?

Although, Data and the EMH were not intentionally designed to trick people into thinking they were real human beings, sometimes they do. Would they pass the Turing Test? Although Data and the EMH appear quite human (more so in the case of the Doctor), this is quite irrelevant in a test where the interrogator cannot see the subject. First, Data would have to fail any natural language test. Yes, he can speak perfect English. But this is his downfall. He is too perfect. Real people do not speak in this way. For example, we learn in *TNG*: "Datalore" that Data cannot speak using abbreviated English. He must pronounce *can't* as *cannot* and *don't* as *do not*. He also has a perfect memory and can calculate at computer-like speed. This type of perfection, while quite impressive to Seven of Nine, would be picked up by a Turing Test interrogator. However, if Data was told about the conditions under which he was about to be tested, he might be sure to type responses that included abbreviations and take his time calculating mathematical questions, thereby faking his real abilities in order to be classified as intelligent.

Another characteristic of Data that would let him down is his ability to process emotions. Originally he was unable to produce emotion of any kind and this was quite evident. When he did install an emotion chip, the emotions were overwhelming and difficult for him to process. This type of behavior, too, would be identified by an interrogator.

The EMH, on the other hand, seems to have a good grasp of colloquial English and his emotional faculties. In *VOY*: "Projections," the Doctor even fools himself when he is confused about whether or not he is a human or a program. He does, however, possess Data's ability to remember events in exact detail (unless someone deletes his memory, as in *VOY*: "Latent Image") and make fast calculations. It is possible that a seasoned interrogator could determine that the EMH was not human. We do conclude, however, that it would be more difficult than catching Data out.

The Turing Test seems to be less of a means of identifying true thinking in machines and more of a challenge to use whatever computable means possible to fool a human into believing the machine is thinking. Turing's philosophy is that we should stop debating the nature of intelligence in machines, and simply say that if you can't tell if it is intelligent or not, then it is.

Even before Turing, and long before computers as we know them, in 1668 Descartes, in his publication, *Discourse on Method*, came up with his own theories about thinking machines:

> *If there were machines which bore a resemblance to our bodies and imitated our actions as closely as possible for all practical purposes, we should still have two very certain means of recognizing that they were not real men. The first is that they could never use words, or put together signs, as we do in order to declare our thoughts to others. For we can certainly conceive of a machine so constructed that it utters words, and even utters words that correspond to bodily actions causing a change in its organs. . . . But it is not conceivable that such a machine should produce different arrangements of words so as to give an appropriately meaningful answer to whatever is said in its presence, as the dullest of men can do. Secondly, even though some machines might do some things as well as we do them, or perhaps even better, they would inevitably fail in others, which would reveal that they are acting not from understanding, but only from the disposition of their organs. For whereas reason is a universal instrument, which can be used in all kinds of situations, these organs need some particular action; hence it is for all practical purposes impossible for a machine to have enough different organs to make it act in all the contingencies of life in the way in which our reason makes us act. [Descartes12]*

What we understand from Descartes is, in brief, that because machines aren't built like us, they cannot think and behave like us, and therefore they will always be identifiable as machines. For example, most primal human motivation is based on bodily urges such as hunger. This is a function of what Descartes refers to as our organs. These organs also produce human emotion, and emotion also drives human behavior. Descartes would therefore be able to tell the EMH apart from a human being because the EMH doesn't eat.

However, just because a machine can be distinguished from a human doesn't preclude it from being intelligent. Turing's original paper, Can Computers Think, began a debate that still rages today.

DISTANT VOICES (*DSN#464*)

The key attribute necessary for passing the Turing Test is for the AI to possess the ability to process natural language. When it comes to Data, the EMH, and many other *Star Trek* AIs, communicating with them through speech seems elementary. However, if you think about the complexities of natural language, considering how they might be programmed is a very challenging topic.

Communicating with natural language is a breeze for humans, but for AI it is entirely a different kettle of fish. Why do you think we use structured languages to program computers? Communicating successfully with natural language (whether spoken or written) requires that both parties (the sender and the receiver) 1) share a common set of symbols and grammars that define the language; 2) share a common context for the communication; and 3) exhibit some signs of rationality[2] [Russell95]. While this form of communication works well using structured programming languages, it isn't as easy with complex natural languages such as English, Chinese, French, etc. Although these languages contain a finite set of symbols and a definable grammar, people do not always adhere to the rules, and what might mean one thing in one context could mean something completely different in another.

There are eight steps involved in communication [Russell95]. We will examine each of these with respect to communicating with Data or the EMH using natural language.

Intention: Communication is first initiated when someone decides to speak[3]. Intention is tightly related to an individual's goals; therefore, the speaker must assume he has something worth communicating and that the hearer will be interested in receiving the communication. When a crew member enters sickbay and hears the familiar, "State the nature of the medical emergency," it is obvious that the EMH's intention is to listen to the symptoms of his patient.

Generation: This is the act of verbalizing the intended information and structuring it according to the rules of the language. It is the process whereby the information in the head of the sender is formed into coherent sentences ready for transmittal. For Data or the EMH this means taking the knowledge that needs to be communicated from their databases and structuring it in a way that the receiver will understand. Often the internal storage of data is not in the form of a natural language sentence, and the speech, therefore, must follow grammatical rules in order to be created.

Synthesis: Speech synthesis is nothing new. Humans can achieve this by passing air over their vocal chords, but computers require complex mathematical equations and programming. We will not be examining the technical aspects of speech synthesis here, but we do know that the EMH and most likely Data have vocal sub-processors. Data is also able to create sound using air, for example, in his attempts to whistle. The EMH, however, is not as fully constructed as Data, and therefore we may assume he has no lungs or even throat.

Perception: As we have already established, perception is the process of receiving some stimuli and converting it into a known internal representation. The perception of speech is a process by which the spoken words are recovered from the communication. As with speech synthesis, computer perception of the spoken word is also a complex set of algorithms and will not be discussed here. To implement speech perception within an AI, speech recognition engines could be integrated with its program. These engines attempt to convert the spoken word into text which can then be interpreted.

Analysis: The process of analysis takes the perceived text and deconstructs it into its primary elements. Deconstructing the text involves using knowledge about the language in order to extract parts pertaining to nouns, verbs, etc. This process is called *parsing*.

Interpretation: Interpretation extracts the meaning of the communication and converts it into a format compliant with the receiver's internal percepts. For Data or the EMH, this would mean converting the text into knowledge that could be inserted into their databases. This type of conversion is called *semantic interpretation*. Often speech can have more than one interpretation. This type of communication is called *ambiguous*. For example, in *VOY:* "Caretaker," the EMH asks Harry for a tricorder. When the EMH realizes that Harry has given him a scientific tricorder when he wanted a medical tricorder, the EMH has to remove the ambiguity from his communication by asking Harry for a medical tricorder. Further interpretation that adds another dimension to the speech is called *pragmatic interpretation* and adds context to the communication with the addition of the situation in which the correspondence was made. In the previous example, Harry wasn't thinking in context when the EMH asked for the tricorder. If he had, he might have assumed the EMH required a medical tricorder.

Disambiguation: This process works by attempting to remove any ambiguities from the communication in order to assess the exact meaning. In the previous example, when the context of being in sickbay is taken into consideration, the communication would probably be interpreted to mean medical tricorder. However, we use the word *probably* here because the communication still may not be clear. So, although it might be possible to remove some ambiguities by selecting the most feasible interpretation, it does not mean that it will always be correct. For example, if B'lanna asked Harry for a tricorder, he might assume an engineering tricorder. The exact same problem exists when humans communicate with each other, so there's no reason that an AI shouldn't get it wrong from time to time.

Incorporation: After the communication has been received and processed, it is added to the AI's database and incorporated with its other knowledge.

One of the more difficult parts of the communication act is the parsing of the given text and breaking it down into its elementary parts ready for interpretation. This process requires extensive knowledge of the language's grammar.

Language Generation and Parsing

Natural language is a complex set of symbols representing characters, words, and punctuation structured according to specific rules called a grammar. In reality, most natural languages are misused by incorrectly spelling words, using colloquial and colorful words, and erroneously constructing sentences. Analysis of the *real* use of the English language, for example, would cause quite a few headaches; therefore, we will examine a more formal and limited version of English to illustrate the parsing process. The syntax we will use to represent the language will be first-order logic.

A simple sentence, *S*, can be considered as the addition of a noun phrase, *NP*, and a verb phrase, *VP*, thus:

$$S \rightarrow NP\ VP.$$

For example, the sentence "I am on the bridge" is constructed from *NP* = "*I*" and *VP* = "*am on the bridge.*" A more complex sentence can be created through the joining of two sentences using a conjunctive keyword (and, or, however, etc.), thus:

$S \rightarrow S$ **and** S	*I am on the bridge and I am not happy.*
$S \rightarrow S$ **or** S	*I am on the bridge or Paris is a Klingon warrior.*
$S \rightarrow S$ **however** S	*I am on the bridge however I need to be in sickbay.*

A noun phrase can be constructed from the following:

- A single noun: Paris, tricorder, warp core, etc.
- A single pronoun: I, me, you, they, etc.
- One or more digits: 3, 85, 214, etc.
- The composition of an <u>article</u> and another **noun**: <u>the</u> **warp core**, <u>a</u> **Vulcan**, etc.
- The composition of a <u>noun phrase</u>, a **preposition** (to, in, on, behind etc.), and another <u>noun phrase</u>: <u>the warp core</u> **in** <u>engineering</u>, <u>a Kazon</u> **behind** <u>the door</u> etc.
- The composition of a <u>noun phrase</u>, "**that**," and a VERB PHRASE: <u>the Kazon</u> **that** IS BEHIND YOU, <u>the Klingon</u> **that** SMELLS, etc.

A verb phrase can be created from the following:

- A single verb: eat, inject, orbit, move, etc.
- A <u>verb phrase</u> and a noun phrase: <u>inject</u> the cordrazine, <u>eat</u> Alterian chowder, etc.
- A <u>verb phrase</u> and an adjective: <u>is</u> injecting, <u>go</u> willingly, etc.
- A <u>verb phrase</u>, a preposition, and a NOUN PHRASE: <u>turn</u> to FACE THE KLINGON, <u>is orbiting</u> near THE QUANTUM SINGULARITY, etc.
- A verb phrase and an adverb: is *orbiting nearby, find the cordrazine here,* etc.

A sentence is easily constructed using a grammar such as the one defined here and a list of nouns, verbs, articles, and more. However, real human language is far more complex. Imagine the extent of the grammar to define the whole of the English language. Then imagine programming all of this into Data or the EMH.

Another effective, and less technical way of processing natural language is by models that don't actually know what they are listening to or talking about. Instead, they statistically analyze the occurrence of words in language and use this information to form communications. These applications don't understand the language they are analyzing and therefore could not really use it. In the next section we will examine a model that analyzes natural language in order to fake some neat communications.

Markov Language Learning

Markov language learning is based on statistics and probability theory. One of the simplest ways of analyzing the essence of a language is called a 2nd order Markov model [Hutchens02]. The model scrutinizes the order in which words occur in sentences and determines the probability that a word will follow a sequence of others. Recall that probability theory, as we discussed in Chapter 4, represents the probability that event A will occur if event B has already occurred, written as follows:

$P(\,A\,|\,B\,)$

The same concept can be used to determine the probability that a word in a sentence will follow a sequence of others. For example, the probability that the words "*medical emergency*" will follow the sequence "*describe the nature of the*" can be written as:

P(*medical emergency* | *describe the nature of the*)

If the value of this probability was 1, we would be able to, with certainty, conclude on hearing the words "*describe the nature of the*" that the next word would be "*medical emergency.*" Now assume you have written a program to work out the probabilities of word sequences. Let's say the program reads the lines:

> *describe the nature of the medical emergency*
> *describe the nature of the warp plasma*
> *describe the nature of Tuvok*

It would set the following probabilities:

P(*medical emergency* | *describe the nature of the*) = 0.333
P(*warp plasma* | *describe the nature of the*) = 0.333
P(*Tuvok* | *describe the nature of the*) = 0.333

Now we turn our idea around and ask the program to generate a sentence in natural language using the probabilities that it knows about word order. We could expect that one third of the time it would generate "*describe the nature of the medical emergency,*" another third of the time it would generate "*describe the nature of the warp plasma,*" and yet another third of the time it would say "*describe the nature of Tuvok.*" As we give the program more and more sentences to learn from, its vocabulary will grow.

A simple implementation of such a program could determine the probability that just one word follows another, for example:

P(*the* | *on*)

The program would have to keep track of each word read and the number of times a particular word has followed it. We took this principal and wrote a simple program, then fed it some quotes from the EMH. In return it produced the following sentences:

```
IT WERE, THAT YOU PUT IT THAT I AM PROGRAMMED WITH CONTINGENCY PRO-
GRAMS UPON PROGRAMS UPON PROGRAMS UPON PROGRAMS AND YOU'LL HAVE
ACCEPTED YOUR PAIN.
GENERALLY, NO, BUT I GAVE NO PERMISSION FOR ANYONE TO DECREASE THE
NEURAL PATHWAY DAMAGE IT WOULD BEST DESCRIBE YOUR STATION.
A SHORT-TERM EMERGENCY SUPPLEMENT TO FIND NEW WAYS TO PATIENTS.
CAPTAIN. IT'S EXTREMELY TECHNICAL.
TISSUE PAPER FOR THE 29-HOUR LEVODIAN FLU.
I AM PROGRAMMED ONLY AS A LIFE.
EXPERIENCE. I HAVE NO NEED FOR ANYONE TO DECREASE THE NEURAL PATH-
WAY DAMAGE IT READY FOR THE MEDICAL PERSONNEL EXPECTED? TRICORDER.
WE'LL SCHEDULE HER FOR THE WHINY, CRANKY ATTITUDES WE SEE AROUND
HERE.
IT APPEARS TO LIVE WITH CONTINGENCY PROGRAMS UPON PROGRAMS AND
DUTIES DO NOT SUBSIDED ON YOUR DOCTOR? POINT FOUR CC'S OF SICKBAY.
THE SENSITIVITY OF THE EMERGENCY HOLOGRAPHIC DOCTOR SPEAKING.
```

And our favorite:

```
I HAD A SHORT-TERM EMERGENCY SUPPLEMENT TO FIND NEW WAYS TO BE
TRANSPORTED OUT OF THE HOLOGRAPHIC RUNNING NOSE.
```

Ok. So they aren't really grammatically correct sentences, but given the simplistic nature of the program that produced them, they aren't half bad. However, as we explained previously, this type of natural language processing does not allow the AI to assign any meaning to what it is saying or what it has processed.

REAL LIFE (*VOY#164*)

In this chapter we have examined a hotly debated topic in AI: the Turing Test. Could *Star Trek* AI pass it? Most definitely! The challenge does not sit with our artificial friends of the 24th century but rather with the contemporary research. Throughout this book we have examined many aspects within the realm of AI; however, we have yet to see any true evolution of being that constitutes a hybrid of technologies sophisticated enough to fool us into believing they are truly alive.

REFERENCES

[Descartes12] René Descartes (*Discourse on Method*), in *The Philosophical Works of Descartes*, Elizabeth Haldane and G.R.T. Ross, translators (Cambridge: Cambridge University Press, 1912), Vol. I, p. 116.

[Hutchens02] Hutchens, J. & Barnes, J., 2002, Practical Natural Language Learning, in S. Rabin (ed) *AI Game Programming Wisdom*, Charles River Media, Hingham.

[Russell95] Russell, S., and Norvig, P., 1995, *Artificial Intelligence: A Modern Approach*, Prentice Hall, Upper Saddle River.

[Turing50] Turing, A., 1950, Computing Machinery and Intelligence, in *Mind*, vol. 59, pp. 433–460.

ENDNOTES

1. Communication in English or some other human language.
2. A common trait of intelligence.
3. We will use speak and speech in referring to both verbal speech and written text (as would be the case in a chat room).

CHAPTER 14

Future's End (*VOY#150,151*)

CHAPTER OVERVIEW

To conclude our look at the artificial intelligences of *Star Trek,* we finish with some discussion on the constraints that should be placed on artificial beings and some lessons we should learn from various *Star Trek* episodes. In addition, we examine a debate between some influential researchers in the AI domain and their views on the plausibility of true AI ever existing.

FUTURE IMPERFECT

As we mentioned earlier, Isaac Asimov specified three laws of robotics in the book *I, Robot*: 1) a robot may not directly or indirectly harm a human being; 2) a robot must obey the directions of a human being except in the case that the orders conflict with 1, and 3) a robot must always protect itself, except where this rule conflicts with 1 and 2. Data, as we learn in *TNG*: "Datalore," was created by Dr. Noonian Soong in an attempt make Asimov's dream of a positronic brain a reality. While Data does not per se adhere to Asimov's robotic laws (he disobeys a direct order in *TNG*: "Measure of a Man") he does have ethical subroutines that essentially prevent him from harming life. The EMH also has ethical and moral subroutines that, first, force him to do no harm (*VOY*: "Latent Image") and, second, compel him to interact with others with essentially human morality and respect.

Worse Case Scenario (*VOY#167*)

The penalty for going against this programming is a systems failure. In *STIX: Insurrection* Data experiences a conflict in his ethical subroutines when he is forced by Starfleet to relocate the entire population of the Ba'ku unbeknownst to them to another planet. After revealing a cloaked duck hide in which Starfleet is secretly spying on the Ba'ku, Data evokes a set of secondary protocols, which we can only assume puts him into a state of self preservation as he evades capture by Starfleet. When eventually Captain Picard and Worf capture Data, La Forge discovers several burned out memory engrams in his positronic brain.

The removal of memory is also a last resort of Captain Janeway in *VOY*: "Latent Image," when the EMH experiences a conflict in his programming when he is made to choose to save one life over another. The conflict occurs because the death of one of his patients goes against the doctor's subroutine which programs him to do no harm. Although in this case it was physically impossible for the EMH to treat both patients, his programming could not resolve the choice he made and his program entered a spiralling downward loop of unresolvable conflict. His behavior becomes erratic just like Data's did in *STIX: Insurrection*.

In the first example, Data's programming conflict is resolved by the removal of the memories causing the problem. He is then asked to retrace his steps by Picard in an attempt to find out what he had known that caused the conflict. As Data relearns about the plot to remove the Ba'ku it does not cause another conflict as Data is not being asked to be part of the plan, but can objectively look at it as an outsider and, with the assistance of the *Enterprise* crew, help to stop it.

In the case of the EMH, the first time the conflict occurs, Janeway simply erases the problem memories. However, the second time, Seven of Nine objects to the doctor being treated in this way and says he should be able to make his own choices. Janeway eventually concurs and babysits the EMH while he attempts to resolve the conflict by reasoning through it. We assume he achieves resolution because he is functioning perfectly in the next *Voyager* episode.

If worse comes to worst in either the behavior of the doctor or Data, their captains always have the option of simply pulling the plug. As demonstrated in *TNG*: "Datalore" and *TNG*: "Message in a Bottle," Dr. Soong built Data with an off switch that totally immobilizes him. In the case of the EMH, it is a simple matter of cutting the power to the computer or mobile emitter running his program.

However, if as AI advocates suggest, artificial beings one day emulate perfect human behavior, they will also possess one of the strongest human motivations: self preservation. This would cause them to do everything in their power to prevent their programs being terminated. As we will see in the next section, having strong human-like motivations could cause serious problems.

Survival Instinct (*VOY#222*)

Koestler [Koestler67], another promoter of the human machine, suggests that human motivation stems from two primary urges: self preservation and species preservation. If one day artificial beings exist to rival humans then surely they must also possess these to motives. Without them, they would be doomed to die out. These goals, of course, may well go against Asimov's laws in that, to fight for their own survival, the machines may have to wipe out their creators.

In VOY: "Prototype," the *Voyager* crew stumble upon an android drifting in space. B'lanna succeeds in repairing its damaged power module. The android introduces itself as Automated Unit 3947 and thanks her for reactivating it. She finds out that the android was created by an extinct race called the Pralor. When the android finds out that B'lanna is able to build new power modules it asks her to build additional modules for other automated units. While the automated units have learned how to repair themselves, the creation of a new power module is beyond their comprehension. Janeway refuses to let B'lanna help the androids *reproduce* as it violates the prime directive. B'lanna is clearly not impressed but submits to Janeway's orders. When Automated Unit 3947 hears this news, it kidnaps B'lanna and forces her to build a prototype android that they can copy and use to rebuild their numbers.

On completing her work another ship manned with similar androids, this type built by the Cravics, turns up and starts attacking the Pralor vessel. B'lanna learns that each race of automated units was created to fight in a war between their creators. Each unit was programmed for victory. When the Pralor and Cravic creators called a truce, the automated units refused to stop fighting and wiped out their creators.

In this example, the creators' orders conflicted with the units' programming. Obviously neither of these races had heard of Asimov's laws. The units refused to let anything get in the way of their goals and this led to the destruction of the very people who had built them.

THE DOOMSDAY MACHINE (*TOS#035*)

Another case of too intelligent AI is illustrated in VOY: "Warhead." In this episode, Harry Kim transports an artificially intelligent warhead suffering from technical amnesia aboard. When the warhead regains its memory, it takes *Voyager* hostage when the crew won't allow it to complete its mission of blowing up a planet. On examining its memory, Harry and B'lanna discover that its launch was a mistake and that the warhead had received a disarm message. The warhead initially refused to believe them saying that they were trying to deceive it. Eventually, Harry persuades the warhead to examine the evidence in its files and it believes him.

In this example we see an AI programmed, as you might expect, to be suspicious of others trying to undermine its goals. The same type of programming is seen in *VOY*: "Dreadnought," which we examined earlier, when B'lanna has to convince a program that she wrote that she was not being coerced to deceive it. These suspicions are indeed something clever to include in an AI's programming in an environment where there might be attempts at implantation of misinformation or propaganda. However, as we can see from all of these examples, the programming must be flexible enough to be able to be reasoned with.

All of these examples also demonstrate a blatant departure from Asimov's laws which could be summarised as *do no harm*. This leads us to suggest our own laws for the future development of AI, though we are not confident others will heed the warning.

1. AIs should obey Asimov's laws or at the very least have ethical subroutines. This means they can by no means be used to destroy any life forms and fight wars on behalf of their creators.
2. AIs should have a fail-safe off switch.

Creating embodied artificial intelligences to fight our own wars seems in the present day to be an unavoidable eventuality. However, those creating them should have the foresight to consider adaptable programming for all possible future scenarios rather than programming simple *destroy at all costs* commands in the heat of battle.

SUDDENLY HUMAN (*TNG#176*)

In this sub-section we pause to examine the question we really want to answer: is AI possible? You will have to excuse us for diverting from *Star Trek* during this section, but all will be forgiven when the *Star Trek* future is reasserted in the next section.

Dreyfus, a Professor of Philosophy at the University of California, Berkeley, wrote a very controversial book called *What Computers Can't Do* [Dreyfus79] in which he said that machines with current-day AI only look intelligent. Indeed, this is all that is required to pass the Turing Test. Dreyfus argues that machines are unable to be intelligent because they are incapable of asking intelligent questions such as why or how, and more importantly, understanding the answers. He also points out that what you see is programmed into them and their output is simply the use of English word tokens used to bridge the gap between their actual output (which at the lowest level would be in binary) and what a human interrogator would understand.

Searle [Searle80] puts forward a thought experiment to dispute the existence of AI called the Chinese Room. Suppose that we have programmed a computer which takes Chinese symbols as input, consults a large database for a match, and outputs other Chinese symbols. Assume this computer performs this task so well that it can convince a human Chinese speaker that it is a Chinese speaker, and it passes the Turing Test with flying colors. Any questions the human asks are responded to appropriately in Chinese. Some would draw the conclusion that the computer understands Chinese.

Next, Searle asks us to imagine an individual sitting inside a small room in which he receives Chinese symbols, looks them up in a table, and returns the Chinese symbols indicated by the table. The individual doesn't understand a word of Chinese, just looks it up in a table. Searle argues that this lack of understanding shows that computers don't understand Chinese either. They are merely programmed with the ability to look information up in a table and match symbols. They can manipulate the symbols but don't actually understand them.

Another opponent of AI is Godel. In his famous Godel's Theorem, he states that AI is impossible because logical systems have limits and because there are some facts that humans can see as true but AI cannot. Godel shows that certain statements can neither be proved nor disproved. For example, consider a truth machine that can answer the truth in any situation. You say to it, "You will never say this sentence is true." Then you ask it, "Was the last sentence true?" If it replies with true, then the sentence must have been false; therefore it would have had to say it was false. If its says that the sentence is false, then in order for it to be false, we would have had to say that it was true, in which case it would have to answer true. Incidentally, this theorem, which stems from the 6th century B.C. philosopher Epimenides' liars paradox, is used by Harry Mudd in *TOS*: "I, Mudd," in an attempt to confuse an android. When the Enterprise crew find themselves hostages of a race of androids, they attempt to confuse the androids and overheat their circuits. To bring the head android, Norman, down, they tell him that Harry Mudd is a notorious liar, who never says anything true. When Norman accepts this, Mudd steps forward and says "I am lying." Norman's circuits fry.

Another academic that uses Godel's Theorem to dispute AI is Roger Penrose [Penrose90]. However, besides taking the stance that AI is just not possible, he suggests that AI is not possible with a logical machine. He instead suggests that what is needed is a quantum machine that is not truth preserving. This machine is based on his theory of the brain which exploits quantum physical effects, believing that the mind should not be considered something working outside the laws of physics but something that should adhere to them.

A theorist who suggests that traditional AI researchers have been going about it the wrong way is Brooks [Brooks91]. Because AI is built using computers, it is the computers' logic that has been used in an attempt to model our understanding of the human brain and the reasoning process. Brooks believes that the key to developing real AI is to study biological intelligence and build systems in a bottom-up manner, for example, starting with a robotic device and gradually adding layers of intelligence rather than the original holistic approach.

On the other side of the coin are the AI advocates. You won't hear them saying that AI has been achieved to date, but you will find them in support of it happening in the future. One such position considers the many billions of years required for nature to develop intelligence and thinking in humans. These people believe it is arrogant to think that humans can replicate these processes in 50 years.

Hugo de Garis, head of the Brain Builder Group at Advanced Telecommunications Research Lab in Japan, believes that they can develop an artificial intelligence far greater that that of a human by using genetic engineering to evolve the software and hardware into systems beyond human comprehension. His goal is to create an artificial brain with a million neuron connections.

Another researcher who disputes the AI critics is Marvin Minsky (a friend of Gene Roddenberry!!). Minsky believes that the concept of mind and consciousness can be explained in terms of a machine [Minsky91]. To the critics who say that these concepts cannot be explained by science,

Minksy rebuts the many people who say that even if a machine were programmed to behave exactly like a human, it could not have subjective experiences. He argues that unless you were actually machine yourself you could not know this. He continues saying that any machine that adequately simulates a human brain would have to produce human behavior. If this is the case, wouldn't it be expected for the artificial being to falsely claim to have consciousness in the same way that we do? For if it was not programmed to behave like a human, then how could it possibly know to make such a claim?

This type of argument that consciousness can be explained by science is also shared by Daniel Dennett [Dennett91] and Hans Moravec [Moravec88]. Dennett postulates that consciousness is an abstraction built from a linear narrative of a person's life. Moravec takes the argument one step further, theorizing that humans are but the first step in a bigger evolution to be succeeded by artificial intelligences. He believes that within 50 years robot intelligences will be able to do everything that humans do and eventually exceed our abilities. They will essentially become bored with us and go off to seek their own fortunes, ultimately inheriting the Earth and the universe.

If you continue along with this type of thinking, the future with AIs seems daunting and uninviting. Indeed, there are many warnings to heed from current day philosophers in terms of the future of AI. These are well demonstrated in numerous *Star Trek* episodes where AIs have gotten out of control.

WHAT YOU LEAVE BEHIND (*DSN#575,576*)

All physical constraints aside, from what you've read in this book, it might seem that artificial intelligences such as those in *Star Trek* are a real possibility. Indeed, there are a lot of projects working on different aspects of AI with some promising results. And although techniques for dealing with uncertainty such as Bayesian inferencing and fuzzy logic brought AI research out of a slump in the mid-1990s, many other problems remain. For example, voice recognition only works in ideal conditions and even then is less than accurate; chess programs are only capable of beating humans because of the structured nature of the game; and robots have trouble negotiating obstacles that we have been able to since we could walk.

The penultimate feat in AI, to program a being such as Data or a virtual being such as the EMH, is such a long way off that we are unable to conclude if by the 24th century such technologies will exist. Such an achievement would take a huge effort and coordination of researchers in all areas of AI. The mind boggles at the immensity of such a task.

In this book we have examined almost every aspect of artificial beings, from their embodiment to their intelligence, and even their soul. While current-day technology will see a human-like android long before the mind is completely programmed, we do not consider that it will be a complete impossibility. With some 330 years before Data is meant to exist in the *Star Trek* future, we indeed have plenty of time to sort out all the issues.

The thought that artificial intelligences might someday inherit the earth is unnerving. Creating beings with such determination and violent natures to self-preserve at any cost seems unnecessary when these types of devices could be used to better our lives and environment. The very nature of AI dictates that researchers look within to discover how we ourselves tick in order to re-create such behavior in machines. This type of research has led to devices that help aid the ability impaired, such as bionic ears, bionic eyes, and physical aids. AI also helps to safely fly planes, land the space shuttle, and explore Mars.

Let's not use it to destroy mankind, but to boldly go where no one has gone before!

REFERENCES

[Brooks91] Brooks, R. A., 1991, Intelligence Without Reason, *Proceedings of 12th Int. Joint Conf. on Artificial Intelligence*, Sydney, Australia, August 1991, pp. 569–595.

[Dennett91] Dennett, D. C., 1991, *Consciousness Explained*, Little Brown & Company, Boston.

[Dreyfus79] Dreyfus, H., 1979, What Computers Still Can't Do: A Critique of Artificial Reason, MIT Press, Cambridge.

[Koestler67] Koestler, A. 1967, *The Ghost in the Machine*, Penguin Books Ltd., London.

[Minsky91] Minsky, M., 1991, Conscious Minds, in *Machinery of Consciousness*, Proceedings, National Research Council of Canada, 75th Anniversary Symposium on Science in Society, June 1991.

[Moravec88] Moravec, H., 1988, *Mind Children: The Future of Robot and Human Intelligence*, Harvard University Press, Cambridge.

[Penrose90] Penrose, R., 1990, *The Emperor's New Mind*, Oxford University Press.

[Searle80] Searle, John, 1980, Minds, Brains, and Programs, *Behavioral and Brain Sciences* 3, 417–424, Cambridge University Press, Cambridge.

Index